EDITING
REALITY TV

EDITING
REALITY TV

THE EASILY ACCESSIBLE
HIGH-PAYING HOLLYWOOD JOB
THAT NOBODY KNOWS ABOUT

JEFF DAWSON

SILMAN-JAMES PRESS   LOS ANGELES

First Edition

10 9 8 7 6 5 4 3 2 1

Library of Congress Cataloging-in-Publication Data

Dawson, Jeff, 1976-
Editing reality TV : the easily accessible, high-paying Hollywood job that nobody knows about / by Jeff Dawson. -- First edition.
pages cm
Includes bibliographical references.
ISBN 978-1-935247-08-1 (alk. paper)
1. Reality television programs--Production and direction. 2. Television programs--Editing. I. Title. II. Title: Editing reality television.
PN1992.8.R43D39 2013
971.45'655--dc23
2013023336

ISBN: 978-1-935247-08-1

Instructional graphics by The Sunset Group

Printed and bound in the United States of America

Silman-James Press
3624 Shannon Road
Los Angeles, CA 90027
www.silmanjamespress.com

For Ali and Beyer, without whom I would not be where I am today. And for my parents.

CONTENTS

PART 2: THE JOB

PREFACE

In the year 2000, REALITY TV hit this country like a juicy, back-stabbing, catfight-filled meteor from television heaven. What was once nothing more than a handful of minor televised anomalies, like a weekly doc about a bunch of MTV kids holed up in a house or a "caught on camera" cop show, suddenly exploded into a pop culture phenomenon. Overnight, terms such as "Rose Ceremony," "Tribal Counsel," and "Head of Household" were permanent fixtures in the nation's lexicon, and the landscape of prime time was chock-full of unbridled, voyeuristic, "real life" television, warts and all. How many people do you know who have made it a tradition to gather around the TV for their nightly dose of *American Idol* or *The Voice*? How many women at the office have you seen feverishly abuzz after an especially shock-filled night on *The Bachelor* or *The Real Housewives*? Reality TV is everywhere. It is all around us. And it is here to stay.

But this revolution has not only changed the viewing experience for the television CONSUMER, it has also completely transformed career potential for the television industry PROFESSIONAL. Suddenly there is a new multibillion-dollar business out there, and with it have come new jobs and the potential for overnight success and limitless fortune. It is the new "Wild West of Entertainment," where the rules are still being written, the kings are still being crowned, and the opportunities are ripe for anyone, anywhere, at any time who has the wherewithal to step up and pluck their prize.

I am writing this book for two reasons. One, I want to share my passion for a new and still evolving craft, a craft that, to my knowledge, has never been discussed in such depth or with such candor. And two, I want to let aspiring visual storytellers everywhere in on a highly CREATIVE, easily ACCESSIBLE, HIGH-PAYING job that NOBODY knows about! This opportunity is Hollywood's best-kept secret—and right now, this minute, it is yours for the taking.

BACKGROUND AND INTRODUCTION

This book is based on my personal experiences in the world of reality TV. It is born of the hundreds of hours I've spent toiling in the trenches, and it is a direct reflection of the many invaluable lessons I've learned along the way. As such, let me start by telling you a little bit about myself and how I came to be—professionally, that is.

I graduated from NYU's Film School in 1999. Like many recent college graduates, I bounced about for that first couple of years, struggling to find my place in the working world. Now admittedly, I wasn't what you might call easy to please. I suffered from the same delusion that might haunt many a naive student who spends four years within the fantasy of the college bubble: I assumed I was an explosion waiting to happen. I figured the moment I stepped out of my cap and gown the world would swoop in from every direction, begging for my talents. I was convinced that I would have my pick of fantastic opportunities and that success, money, and power would be an immediate and overnight given.

In my defense, I did at least have some sense of focus. I knew I wanted to work in the entertainment industry. I wanted to move to Hollywood and to be a part of the fantasy factory I had spent my entire life daydreaming about. But determining in what capacity I would realize this dream proved a bit more challenging...

I liked writing and storytelling, so I tried my hand at screenwriting. I enjoyed bossing people about, so I took a stab at directing. I loved to perform, so I gave acting a go. But with high expectations for immediate success and so little patience for anything less, my attempts at the Hollywood dream quickly floundered. Nothing seemed to go as planned. No matter what I tried, I kept finding myself in the exact same place—a nobody performing menial tasks for no money and very little professional reward. To make matters worse, I was again and again catering to the whims of self-important Hollywood jerks who treated me like anything but the overnight wunderkind I imagined myself to be. Despair soon followed. It began to seem as if Hollywood success might not be in the cards for me.

But that was all about to change, and in the most unexpected of ways.

While I muddled about with my less-than-encouraging stabs at success, something big was happening in the world of television. Something new had arrived from across the Atlantic. In early 2000, producer Mark Burnett helped bring the popular international reality series *Survivor* to the US. It was an immediate ratings behemoth, and a brand-new form of American television was born in an instant. This is not to say that reality television of a sort had not existed in the US prior to *Survivor*. MTV's *The Real World*, ABC's *America's Funniest Home Videos*, and the syndicated *COPS* had been around for years. (And old-fashioned game shows and talent shows existed in TV's earliest days.) However, *Survivor* was the first serialized documentary-style TV program to hit a mass audience with such immediate and record-breaking success. Within a year the networks were rolling out reality TV like crazy: *The Bachelor, Big Brother, American Idol, The Apprentice,* and *Dancing with the Stars*—shows that found hungry audiences and huge ratings.

Around this time I made my last desperate attempt at "living the dream": EDITING! I had been lucky enough to pick up some editing skills while in school and was able to leverage these into a job. But the employment I found was as an ASSISTANT editor, not an editor. And my first assignment—a low-budget horror movie—barely covered my rent, let alone things like food, clothing, and gas. Again, not exactly the illustrious work I had hoped for. Also, as an assistant editor, I was responsible for the technical side of editing, not the creative. To excel in this position one needs to be organizationally sound, computer savvy, and a fan of sacrificing late nights and weekends. Well, at the time I was computer illiterate, an unabashed slob, and an absolute lover of sleep. Suffice it to say, I wasn't a perfect fit, so I soon became discouraged and prepared to throw in the towel.

It seemed I was finally out of options. Maybe it truly was time to give up my dreams and settle into life as a Hollywood failure. But as the Rolling Stones song so wisely preaches: *"You can't always get what you want. But if you try sometimes, you just might find you get what you need."*

When I was at my lowest and ready to book a ticket home, I got "THE CALL"! On the other end was a post supervisor by the name of Rusty Austin. He had an offer. He was working on a new reality series for Fox called *Anything for Love* and needed a strong, competent assistant editor to help usher the series through postproduction. My first thought was, "Competent? Usher? Jeez, he must have the wrong number!" Then he told me the pay: $1,100 a week. That was more than double what I was making in the bowels of low-budget horror. In fact, that was more than I had made on any job doing anything ever! I couldn't say no. And I'm glad I didn't, because what I stepped into was not just another gig, it was an entirely new world. It was the beginning of the rest of my professional life.

Reality TV, I quickly learned, plays by very different rules than movies and scripted television. It's an editor's medium. Although technically there is no script, there is still a story to be told, and that story needs to be written. The difference is that the writing is now being done in post, on the computer—THROUGH THE EDITING. As such, the editor is king! Editors are catered to, respected, and, best of all, much in demand! They are also among the most highly paid people in the reality business. A single reality TV show is often derived from days, even weeks of raw material. With so much footage and often very tight deadlines, the shows are constantly in need of more and more editors. Because of this, assistant editors who might work for a decade to get a bump in the scripted world are promoted to editor within a year, sometimes even sooner.

Here it was: everything that I naively thought I would just walk right into—money, rapid promotion, creative power, and respect—and I had actually WALKED RIGHT INTO IT! Suffice it to say, my formerly disorganized, sleep-loving, tech-averse self did a 180.

Within nine months I was an editor, and once again my salary more than doubled. By the end of the following year I had gone from making $26,000 a year in low-budget features to more than $150,000 a year editing reality TV. I became a condo owner at 26 and a Hollywood Hills homeowner at 31. And the truth is it really wasn't that hard. Sure I worked diligently. I paid my dues on the night shift and put in the extra hours as I refined my skills, but I had a hell of a lot of fun doing it. I was MAKING TV! And best of all, I was able to ride this career rocket to the top while working with and for NICE PEOPLE. Reality TV, perhaps because it is such a new and fresh-faced industry, has managed to escape many of the superficial, self-important trappings of old-school Hollywood. These are people who don't posture and patronize with delusional self-obsessed Hollywood arrogance. They don't stab you in the back, belittle you in the halls, or throw their coffee in your face because it doesn't have their favorite brand of fat-free organic soymilk. They respect you and allow you to do your job. That's it.

Over the past decade I have worked on dozens of reality shows for many of the biggest networks. I have had a significant hand in shaping hundreds of hours consumed by millions of viewers. I have made a true impact on the television landscape and continue to do so. I am now proud to say that I am truly at the top of my game. I am paid more than many of my peers and have one of the most enviable jobs in the business. I have managed to achieve all of my Hollywood dreams in a way I could never have imagined when I first arrived in Hollywood. In the end, that naive college graduate was somehow proven right after all.

• • •

So there's my story. Why do I tell it? Because every time I do I am shocked to see how many people find it so hard to believe. And I guess that's why I call this Hollywood's best-kept secret to success. Nobody tells you that with a little focus and hard work you can go from nothing to making $200,000 a year in no time. Nobody tells you that you don't need to go to film school or get an agent or serve coffee to self-obsessed Hollywood jerks to get ahead in show business. All you need is energy, focus, and the tools that I am about to set forth for you in this book.

This is not a technical text. It will not teach you how to use the Avid or Final Cut Pro or any other editing device. A lot of that stuff you can learn on the job. What I am offering you here is something much more valuable than keystrokes and file menus: I'm offering you the best possible approach and path to success in a medium that is growing faster than almost any other in the entertainment industry.

So, good luck. Pay attention, and I'll see you in the editing bays.

PART 1
THE CRAFT

BEFORE WE BEGIN:

GUESS WHAT? YOU'RE REALLY A WRITER!

As part of writing this book I sat down with a number of my most respected colleagues and collaborators. I interviewed top reality editors, directors, and producers. I grilled them all on the many dimensions of reality TV editing and allowed their experiences and perspectives to inform my approach. Of all the important points and precious insights imparted, there was one I felt so strongly about that I've decided to give it its own "pre-chapter." I firmly believe that no discussion of reality TV editing can begin without first discussing the concept of WRITING REALITY. The reason is simple: that is precisely what a reality TV editor does. We are not just assemblers, shapers, trimmers, refiners, and stream-liners. Sure, we do all of that, but first and foremost a great reality TV editor is a STORYTELLER.

In the entertainment industry, reality TV is referred to as "unscripted" television. The obvious definition for this would be television without a script. Television without a script? Really? Do you actually believe that reality TV is scriptless? That would mean that content just HAPPENS to play out as a perfect, clear, and concise series of events before the camera. And that upon return from the field (or wherever it's shot) it makes total sense and tells a complete and fulfilling story, without any need for adjustment or alteration. YEAH, RIGHT! Do you really think that Kim Kardashian's life just "falls into place" before the camera without distractions, tangents, and diversions? Do you really think The Real Housewives are immune to the unpredictable chaos of life that can alter and distort a strong story at every turn? Of course not. It's hard enough to competently capture a script when there actually IS one. Trying to capture a clear, balanced, and fulfilling narrative (i.e., your story) WITHOUT a script is nearly impossible. So, no, "unscripted" television does NOT mean television without a script. What the industry really means by "unscripted" television is that it is a form of television that doesn't hire or pay for writers. It doesn't need to; that's our job.

Unscripted television HAS a script. It just isn't written in the same way that traditional narrative entertainment is. If you make scripted television or film, dialogue, action, dramatic revelations, and heartfelt conclusions would all be devised, drafted, and refined on paper before a tripod is broken out or a frame is focused. In reality it's just the opposite. Yes, there is some level of story preparation that goes into planning a shoot. There is a way that the producers would LIKE things to go. But, for the most part, reality is just that—reality. The cameras roll and things happen. It's unpredictable and impossible to truly control. I know this because I've worked on both sides. I've been in the field. I've directed and produced. I know that no matter how much you prep and how much you try to control, what you actually get on tape has everything to do with the WHIMS OF FATE.

> *"We're solving puzzles all day long and that's the allure...well, that and the check."*
>
> Jackson Anderer, Editor
> *Extreme Makeover: Home Edition* and *Celebrity Apprentice*

Have you ever heard the line "We'll fix it in post?" Well, in reality TV, it goes a bit more like "We'll MAKE IT in post." We reality television editors carry the weight of a show's clear and concise beginning, middle, and end on our shoulders. We bear the responsibility for story development, character evolution, and dramatic progression. We ARE the writers of reality TV.

So why is this scripting point so crucial that I've chosen to open the book with it? Because a reality TV editor must always, always, always look at his work from a WRITER's perspective. Every choice you make, every cut, every dissolve, every effect needs to be in the service of the story YOU are responsible for telling. You need to constantly ask yourself story questions: Where has this character come from? Where is she going?

How does this scene support the next? What is the conclusion I am building toward? And MOST importantly: Have I found the most engaging, dramatic, energetic, and captivating way to tell my story? It's on your shoulders. You, and only you, can deliver the goods to the world.

Before we move on, I want to acknowledge that there are others aiding you in your pursuit. I don't mean to discount the many producers who work hard to prep a production, manage shoots, and guide your progress in post. These are talented collaborators, and I have worked with and learned from the best of them. Their incredible contributions are often invaluable to the process, but that should by no means alter your perspective. Producers can only do so much for the editor. They can help inform the bigger picture and suggest overall focus, but they cannot MAKE your scene for you. At the end of the day they must walk away, your door must close, and you must dive into the footage alone. And when the producer returns, he or she expects to see *a dramatic, captivating story*, not just assembled footage.

REALITY TV: FROM CONCEPT TO SCREEN

As we go through the many concepts within this book, we will draw our examples from actual reality TV shows and discuss the various steps that go into making them. To start off, I'll give you a brief basic rundown of how an episode of a popular reality show goes from concept to screen. Let's take Oxygen's *Tori and Dean: Home Sweet Hollywood* as our model.

PREPRODUCTION

This is the pre-shoot preparation period. It takes place before the cameras roll. It can last anywhere from one to four weeks, sometimes longer. **Preproduction** is essentially the producer's domain. During this time, *plot ideas* will be spitballed and storylines will be developed. What's coming up in the lives of Tori and Dean? Are there any big or interesting events: weddings, birthdays, visits, or visitors? If nothing obvious is on the horizon, can we orchestrate anything big or interesting: renewing vows, date night, a surprise party, etc.?

Once a handful of plot ideas (enough to cover a season's worth of television) are chosen, preparations for shooting will commence. Producers will work on securing necessary locations and permits. They will design a shooting schedule and begin hiring a production crew. The line producer will begin approving expenditures and monitoring an often tight budget. And the casting department will swing into action, selecting the people who will surround Tori and Dean and color the scenes. Yes (I'm sorry to reveal), this stuff is rarely left to chance. It simply can't be. The last thing you want is to be saddled with a supporting cast of complete bores.

PRODUCTION

This segment of the process is the domain of producers, cameramen, sound mixers, and various other below-the-line assistants. Together they form the *crew*. For a show like *Tori and Dean*, a single episode will often be captured in less than a week, probably four to five days, and normally the crew will shoot as many episodes as possible back-to-back.

There's an old saying: "Men plan, God laughs." This is a most apropos description of reality TV's **Production** phase. I've said it before, and I promise that I will say it again and again: *Reality is extremely unpredictable.* This is real life. There is no script. The crew may go out with a general notion of what is to happen. There may even be some pre-planned obstacles to ensure conflict. But for the most part the drama will be unexpected and unplanned, and it is the job of a competent production crew to remain flexible enough to follow that drama wherever it goes. It is their charge to capture everything and anything they can to provide the editor with as many dramatic options as possible.

POSTPRODUCTION

Once the producers and their shot tapes have returned from the field, the last process—**postproduction**—begins. Usually the first week or so of postproduction is editor free. Things need to be prepped before editors can actually start editing. The footage has to be ingested, broken down, labeled and organized, and *field notes* must be generated to help guide the process. (Field notes are a written account of what was captured during the shoot, including what relates to the initial plan, and what additional moments of dramatic gold transpired.)

By week two, though, with the footage in and shoot documented, it's time to start cooking. Enter the editor! As I've said, it is the job of the editor, aided by producers and field notes, to explore, find, and WRITE the show. If the show is an hour long, he or she will generally have four to five weeks to deliver a first "rough cut" of an episode to the network. (If the show is a half-hour long, the editor will only have two to three weeks to deliver a first rough cut.) Sometimes one editor will be responsible for one entire episode and will create its entire experience scene by scene. More often, a group of editors will work together to build each episode, and this is the setup that we will assume to be the standard throughout this book.

Each editor will be assigned a handful of individual scenes to construct, addressing the producer's notes as he works. Finished scenes will be handed off to one editor in the group, often the most seasoned. This editor, the *finishing editor*, will link together the various scenes in proper order, build them into *acts*, and begin polishing the episode as a whole. (As we all know, commercial television does not play as a ceaseless experience. A TV show is made up of a series of *acts*, which are like chapters in a book. Separating one act from another are the show's commercial breaks. Normally, an hour-long show has six of these breaks and a half-hour show has three or four.)

When the episode has been assembled, broken into acts, and polished, it will then be sent to the network, in this case Oxygen. Generally, a network will require two rough cuts (complete but rougher edits) and a "fine cut" (more polished final edit) over a two week period. This basically means they get to look at the show three times, and each time generate a series of notes to be addressed by the editors.

After the network is satisfied with the episode, it will be designated "approved." This signals the finishing editor's final responsibility in the process, *locking the show*. This simply means bringing the show to its exact running time. (Every TV episode has an exact running time that is dictated by the network. For a half-hour show the running time is around 22 minutes; for an hour it is around 44 minutes.)

Once the show is locked it is then handed off, often to a third-party audio or video finishing company, for final technical adjustments. I will cover this in more detail later in the book, but for now, just know that this stage involves bringing the picture and sound up to refined television standards and then delivering all of the elements necessary for the network to air the show.

So there you go. Those are the basics of the process. Many of these points will be covered in greater detail in later chapters. For now, though, I think you have what you need to move forward.

Throughout the following chapters you will find small gray boxes (such as this one) entitled **"In the Bay."** These are practical, on-the-job examples that help illustrate the ideas discussed in the text.

NOTE: Reality TV shows are built one scene at a time. So, in the following chapters, I will first walk you through a simple, direct, and concise approach to editing a great scene. The first three chapters will guide you through the process of assembling the first rough cut: how to approach raw (i.e., unedited) footage, how to select material from that footage, how to outline your scene based on your selections, and, finally, how to assemble your selected footage into your outlined scene. Chapters 4–10 discuss ways to accentuate and improve upon the scenes you assemble (via manipulating footage and using interviews, music, and sound effects). Chapters 11–12 include additional information and advice about the process.

CHAPTER 1

HAVE A PLAN

"You cannot edit if you have no story to tell. Editing starts with story. And story starts with a plan."

Bill Marin, Editor,
Nanny 911 and *Catfish: The TV Show*

GETTING STARTED

The first element that every editor must deal with on any reality job—well, frankly, any editing job *period*—is RAW FOOTAGE. Raw footage is the uninterrupted sound and picture as it was captured on location by the production crew. In reality TV, raw footage is basically lightly produced documentary video. It is often random, technically erratic, and VERY, VERY, VOLUMINOUS!

A reality editor may step into an assignment with tens of hours of footage on his or her plate, sometimes even hundreds! There could be days, even weeks of haphazardly shot material to navigate through and cobble into minutes of focused story, and often this footage will be captured by multiple cameras simultaneously. Needless to say, raw footage can be an intimidating beast to behold, not to mention time-consuming.

It is because of this that no editor should ever begin his or her process, and I certainly never begin mine, without first having a PLAN. After all, editing a multimillion-dollar television series usually involves very tight deadlines. Time is money for everyone involved, so you need a plan of attack if you want to keep up and keep your paycheck.

THE MEANING OF A PLAN

Okay, great, so you need a plan. But what does that mean? Well, let's step away from editing for a second and talk about something a little more everyday—like grocery shopping. Let's also get a little more specific, add some stakes, give it context, something comparable to the deadlines and weight of a television editing job.

Let's say you have a hot dinner date. Maybe it's a first date with that special someone you've been chasing for a while. You've invited your date to your home for an evening of fine dining and magnetic company. This is your one shot and you don't want to screw it up!

But there's a problem. You're running late at work. And you still need to buy the food, get home, shower, change into something snazzy, and actually fix the meal, so you don't have much time to waste at the grocery store. You can't just wander the aisles willy-nilly and let the shelves inspire your palate. There are too many options, too many wrong turns and dead ends.

So, before you step into the fray, you need to have a meal PLAN (your menu) in mind. You need to know the dish you want to make; only then can you enter that grocery store of possibilities with the focus necessary to get what you need and get out in time for your date.

In editing, the PLAN is not a dish, but it isn't too far off. Amid all of the details, left turns, and tangents that make up reality's raw footage, the PLAN is the simple A+B=C storyline that you set out to tell. It is the outline, the skeleton, or the spine of your scene. Just as knowing your dish's required ingredients will allow you to remain focused in the grocery store, a strong scene plan will keep you on point as you navigate that scene's raw footage. It will guide you in assessing what footage is essential and what is merely a distraction, serving only to slow the process and confuse the end product.

• • •

Okay, now that we know what a plan is, how do we go about making one? Among the many hours of raw footage from which any number of stories might be told, how do you determine which story will best serve your show?

KNOW THE BIGGER PICTURE

In order to even begin thinking about the story you want to tell with your raw footage, you first have to have a sense of the BIGGER PICTURE. You need to understand the show's larger story and how the scene you are about to edit can play into it. To grasp this, you must first determine three overriding things: the show's **Story Arc**, **Character Arcs**, and **Theme**.

Story Arc

A story arc is a plot's trajectory from start to finish. It is the storyline of the episode and/or series that is set up in the opening, supported throughout the show, and resolved at the end. For an episode of *Survivor*, it could be the demise and elimination of a "survivor," including all of the trip-ups and fallout scenes that build toward the elimination and result from it. On *Real Housewives* it could be a housewife's extravagant birthday bash, starting with the many obstacles and prep scenes that lead up to it and ending with the bash's final resolution and aftermath.

In the Bay:

You are editing an episode of *Big Brother*, and you know that a player will be betrayed down the line by his closest allies. How might your scene help to build toward this conclusion? How might you help to tell this story? Perhaps within your raw footage is that initial secret meeting where his allies agree to betray him. Or perhaps you have the scene where he commits the crime that turned his allies against him in the first place.

If it's a show such as *Top Chef*, and you know that a competitor is going to be eliminated, what trip-ups are made within your raw footage that could support this fate? In your raw footage, any number of competing chefs might make any number of mistakes, but to serve the larger **Story Arc**, you need to hit on the soon-to-be-eliminated character's one best trip-up that will play out down the road.

Whether you are cutting a "self-contained" show, in which each episode presents a complete story with no cliffhangers (*Extreme Makeover: Home Edition*, *Intervention*, *Undercover Boss*), or a "serialized" show in which an interconnected story builds from episode to episode throughout the series (*The Bachelor*, *Survivor*, *Top Chef*), as an editor you will always be dealing with a storyline that is much bigger than your single scene. For this reason, as you decide how to cut a scene you must always ask yourself: What is the dramatic payoff in the end (of the episode and/or series), and how could my scene help to set it up or pay it off?

Character Arc

Much like the story arc traces the beginning, middle, and end of a plot line, a character arc traces the beginning, middle, and end of a character's journey of transformation (for better or worse) through a story. It will begin with a character's introduction. How does a character make his or her entrance to a show? What actions, impressions, and testimonials shape this introduction? Then, as the story progresses, how might the character evolve? What actions, reactions, and changing opinions influence this evolution? In the end, who does this character prove to be? How does this character transform? What transforms him? What is his ultimate fate, and how does this affect every other character and the story as a whole?

In the Bay:

If you are editing a dating show like *Rock of Love with Bret Michaels*, you must know the trajectory of each woman's **Character Arc** throughout the series. How is each character to be perceived as the show progresses? How might your scene serve to develop this perception? Who are you developing into the villain? Who are you building to be the fan favorite? Who will be your red herring? Obviously, how a woman is perceived—initially and throughout her transformational journey—is incredibly important on a show like *Rock of Love*. This will not only affect her relationships with others, but also justify her fate.

Developing strong **Character Arcs** is the ultimate way to humanize your material for the audience. We want to relate to the character on the screen. We want to see ourselves in that character and be able to project our personal experiences into the world of the show. It's nice to see Joe lose weight, but to watch him transform into a stronger, more confident man because of his weight loss captivates us. It's cool to watch a bunch of volunteers renovate a house, but to watch a needy family given a new lease on life by this renovation can be riveting.

Theme

Sometimes, in addition to a story arc and numerous character arcs, you may also need to support a show's overall theme, a central message that plays into every episode, every season, and is a large part of the show's identity.

For example, the competition show *The Biggest Loser* is a show about healthy living. Healthy living is its theme. Whether it is a training scene, a competition or a weigh-in, this theme is always present. The competitors and viewers are constantly being reminded of the choices they can make to lose weight, stay healthy, and change their lives for the better. Therefore, as you assess the raw footage and structure your plan, you should always be looking for opportunities to support this theme and, ultimately, the overall identity of the show.

Take Note: Big Picture Resources (a.k.a. Producers)

We've discussed what constitutes the Bigger Picture—the theme and story and character arcs. We've established how crucial it is to have this handle on a show before forming a scene's editing plan and diving into the raw footage. But how exactly do we go about getting this handle? Luckily, on most productions there are readily available resources to help us fill in this crucial blank: They are called PRODUCERS.

There are many types and levels of producer, and often their titles and responsibilities shift from show to show. I've worked on big network shows with dozens of producers available to you at any time, and I've worked on tiny cable shows that might have one or two producers for ten editors or more. I've had jobs where the producer will check in with you (sometimes even sit beside you) through every step of the process, and I've had others where I might see the producer only once or twice throughout the whole process.

Every show and every experience is different, but there is one constant: Producers are there to help guide the show to completion. It is their job to keep its overall vision (the bigger picture) on track. Therefore, the producers are the ones that you, as the editor, must connect with before your plan making can begin in earnest. It is their job to apprise you of the arc of the story, and if there isn't an apparent one, it is their job to help you find it.

KNOW THE "RAW"

Having a firm handle on a show's bigger picture is key, but it does us no good unless we have an even firmer handle on the material—the raw footage (which TV folk often simply call the "raw")—that we have to work with in the first place. Reverting to one of my earlier analogies, you can't choose your meal's recipe without some general knowledge of what's in the grocery store. Likewise, you can't construct the best story unless you know what your story options actually are. You need an overview of the events and a rundown of the action. In short, you need to KNOW THE RAW, and there are three avenues for discovering this: *Field Notes*, *Field and Story Producers*, and the *Watch Down*.

Field Notes

This is a document, or compiled group of documents, describing the moments of action captured by the camera. Often, the field notes will highlight key story points and give you a reference for where to locate them within the footage. By carefully reviewing the field notes, not only will you get a feel for the raw overall, you can also quickly identify key dramatic moments that might work together to tell a strong and big picture–appropriate story.

On the next page is an example of what the field notes might look like for a day of production on a fictional reality show called *Single Gals*.

"Single Gals"
Field Notes
Date: **April 2, 2014**

Producer(s): Jerry Jones	Episode # **107**
Camera Op(s): Mike Miller, Sara Wilson	Shoot Day # **2**
Sound Op(s): Peter Garrison	Location: The Grove, Los Angeles, CA

Events:
J&T arrive at The Grove
J&T shop at Nordstrom and discuss love life
J&T get coffee and discuss speed-dating

Time Code	Cam/Load	Beat
		TAPE 040213A01 - 040213B01
12:32:00	Cam A	ESTABLISHING SHOTS. The Grove shopping center.
		PARKING GARAGE
12:34:52	Cam A/B	JOANNE and TINA exit their car in parking garage and move to the escalator.
		ESCALATOR.
12:36:41	Cam A/B	JOANNE and TINA descend discussing TINA'S recent blind date. TINA is upset that he made her split the bill. JOANNE can't believe it either. "What a loser!" GOOD ENERGY
12:38:16	Cam A/B	JOANNE and TINA move across the outdoor grounds towards Nordstrom entrance.
12:41:18	Cam A/B	JOANNE and TINA enter Nordstrom.
		NORDSTROM MAKEUP COUNTER
12:44:40	Cam A/B	JOANNE and TINA browse the Nordstrom makeup counter. They laugh about JOANNE'S divorce and how happy she is to finally be free of her philandering ex.
12:48:46	Cam A/B	TINA asks a SALESPERSON to try a new foundation cream.
12:56:10	Cam A/B	TINA buys the cream
13:00:13	Cam A	BROLL - various shots of makeup display. CU on foundation cream in case.
		NORDSTROM PURSE AISLE
13:10:58	Cam A/B	JOANNE and TINA are browsing purses.
13:16:25	Cam A/B	JOANNE and TINA model various purses. They laugh about the sad state of single men these days. "Have guys always sucked this much?" FUNNY.
13:18:27	Cam A	CUT AWAY – CU of JOANNE'S hand holding black purse.
13:22:25	Cam A	BROLL various purses on display.
		"IN-STORE" STARBUCKS
13:34:54	Cam A/B	JOANNE and TINA are in line at the "in-store" Starbucks. TINA asks JOANNE if she has ever tried speed-dating. "Absolutely not!!! Are you kidding???" TINA thinks they should. They debate the issue. GOOD ENERGY.
13:42:58	Cam A/B	They pause the debate to order drinks.
13:44:28	Cam A/B	JOANNE insists on paying and Tina feigns resistance but quickly accepts.
13:50:29	Cam A/B	JOANNE and TINA wait for their drinks. TINA starts in again on speed-dating.
13:54:00	Cam A/B	After another lengthy debate, JOANNE agrees to consider it.
14:00:08	Cam A/B	JOANNE and TINA exit Nordstrom and walk off camera.
14:03:33	Cam A/B	Room Tone of Nordstrom interior
14:06:38	Cam A	BROLL - store signage.
14:08:25	Cam A	PICKUP - car pulling in/out of parking spot.

Field and Story Producers

As I said before, producers are your most valuable collaborators and guides. They are there to help navigate the story underlying each and every scene you are assigned, and they are a great resource when determining WHAT EXISTS IN THE RAW. Sometimes they will be the field producers, who actually helped capture the footage and helped generate the above-mentioned field notes. Other times they will be postproduction story producers who were absent from the set but have since spent hours viewing and absorbing the footage to give you a head start. Both of these producers have often already identified the important story points, and thus are invaluable in guiding you toward the creation of your plan.

The Watch Down

If there are no story producers or field notes to assist you, you will have to take on the task of "watching down" the raw footage yourself. This watch down is by no means the beginning of your physical edit. It is strictly for the purpose of getting to know WHAT YOU HAVE. Grab a piece of paper, a cup of coffee, and a strong sense of the bigger picture, and start watching. Write down each important action or shift in drama as it occurs. If you feel you've missed something, go back and watch the material again. Your goal is to generate a play-by-play synopsis of the raw footage. Essentially, YOU are writing up the field notes. Only after you have scanned the footage and noted its contents in detail, and then reviewed your notes, should you start to identify your editing plan, just as you would if actual field notes existed.

GIVE IT A LOGLINE

Once you've assessed the bigger picture and digested the raw, it's time to choose your story's focus, to select the story you wish to tell with your footage. In short, it's time to make your editing plan. And, as any good industry writer knows (remember, you're a writer), every good story starts with a strong **Logline**.

A logline is a simple, concise explanation that sums up the basic story of the scene. It should be written out in as few words as possible and serve as a succinct reminder of your overall story focus throughout the editing process.

As a reality TV editor, forcing yourself to focus your story with a logline will keep you on point as you navigate the raw. If we were to compare it with the grocery shopping analogy, the logline would be the name of your dish, for instance, "spaghetti and meatballs." This is a simple and succinct summation of the end goal. It will keep you focused and on task as you make your way through the grocery store.

For the purposes of editing, though, let's come up with a more narrative and TV-appropriate example. Let's imagine we have a sense of our bigger picture and we've been given a heap of raw footage and a handle on what went down during its shooting. From these, we've decided upon the best story to tell within our scene, for which we've derived the following logline:

"GUY MEETS GAL IN CLUB AND GETS HER NUMBER."

This is a clear and concise statement of what the story is about. It is a focused description of the goal we are setting out to achieve and the basic information we are trying to convey. This is THE STORY of our scene. It tells you the characters and the action of the scene. It tells you how the scene will begin and how it will end. It will keep you on track and help streamline the process of navigating the raw.

So, What Now?

We have a strong plan, and we have summarized it with a succinct and focused logline. So now what do we do? Well, like I said, the logline is the name of our dish. We know the meal we want to make. Now we need to start shopping for its ingredients—or, as this process is called in reality TV editing, **PULLING SELECTS**.

CHAPTER 1 REVIEW

Choose the correct answers from the lettered list.

1. ___ _____ is the first element that every editor must deal with on any reality job.

2. No editor should ever begin his or her process without first having a ___.

3. In order to determine your plan of attack, you must have a sense of the _____ and a handle on what went down in the _____.

4. To properly determine the bigger picture, you must first assess and determine the _____ ___, _____, and _____.

5. The _____ are the best resources for determining the bigger picture.

6. What are the three avenues for determining what went down in the "raw"?

7. Once you have settled on a plan, or the basic story of your scene, what does every good industry writer know to create next?

    a. A logline
    b. Raw footage
    c. Bigger picture
    d. A plan
    e. Story arc, character arc, theme
    f. Field notes, field or story producers, the watch down
    g. Producers

Answers: 1-b, 2-d, 3-c, 4-e, 5-g, 6-f, 7-a

WATCH AND LEARN

Throughout this book I will stress again and again the importance of practical hands-on research. And by this I mean TUNING IN and TAKING NOTE (i.e., carefully studying/watching what others have already done in your chosen field). So fire up that DVR, load that Hulu page, and start streaming Netflix, because it's time to get up close and personal with some reality TV.

1. Grab a recorded episode of your favorite reality show, a piece of paper, and a pen. Watch the entire show from start to finish. Once you're done, go back to the beginning and start again. This time I want you to pause at the end of each scene and try to imagine what that scene's **Plan** was. Now, challenge yourself to define that plan in the form of a **Logline**. Try to boil each scene down to its absolute essence. Some will be easier than others, but the more you work at it, the better you'll be.

2. For this exercise I want you to select a different reality show episode to watch. Fast-forward to its last five minutes and press PLAY. Watch the last few scenes all the way to the credits. Once you're done, roll back to the top of the episode and start watching it from the beginning. Now, as you watch, note any time in any scene where something is being SET UP or STRESSED that will be paid off in the last five minutes that you've already reviewed. Are competitors and their screw-ups being featured to set up certain characters for an eventual elimination? Are relationships being strained for an eventual blowout? Are suspicions being planted for an eventual revelation? What I think you'll find is that, more often than not, scenes will exist in large part to serve an episode's last five minutes. Early scenes build toward a conclusion, an outcome. They serve the **bigger picture.** Check it out. See for yourself. Watch and learn.

CHAPTER 2

DIGGIN' FOR GOLD

I like to think of reality as sculpting story with found objects.

When I was young my family would vacation on an island in Maine. It was a fairly remote island with very little in terms of modern entertainment. There were no movie theaters or malls; there wasn't even a local public pool. Now, for many, this kind of escape would be a perfect way to decompress. But for a couple of pent-up, overstimulated adolescents like my sister and me, this could be torture! We needed constant distraction, and it fell to my mother to make that happen. She had to create activities to keep us occupied. She had to manufacture games and adventures that would keep us out of her hair and out of trouble.

Our favorite of these activities was something my mom dubbed "The Great Sea Glass Treasure Hunt." If you aren't familiar with sea glass, it is small glass shards that have been tumbled by the sea for years. When they finally wash up on the shore they are as smooth as pebbles. But unlike pebbles, sea glass comes in any number of cool colors, including blue, red, orange, and green. And when gathered into a pile, these colorful gems truly resemble the shimmering bounty of a pirate's treasure chest (or at least a 10-year-old boy's concept of what that might look like).

The rules of the game were simple. My sister and I were to scour the beach looking for this glimmering glass, and whoever found the most would win a special prize. The reward was generally money for candy, or perhaps control over the TV remote that evening. And given that we both LOVED candy and each had VERY different television tastes, the game was most definitely ON!

Now, the process of finding sea glass is a challenging one. It's not as if you go to a beach and it's just strewn with the stuff, not at all. It's hidden.

There are only so many pieces to find, and they are often mixed together with and camouflaged by rocks, shells, sand, and seaweed. It takes absolute focus and a very careful eye to uncover the gems. You have to scour the beach, leaving no spot unturned or uninspected. Then, once you've scoured every inch, SCOUR IT AGAIN AND AGAIN.

In reality TV editing, we have our own version of "The Great Sea Glass Treasure Hunt." It's called **PULLING SELECTS**, the process of discovering the best raw footage moments from which to build a scene.

Think of your raw footage as that beach of sand, rocks, and shells. You need to search for your story gems with the same focus and intensity as I scoured for my pieces of glass treasure. You must thoroughly review and examine every moment of the raw material. It will take focus, time, and patience. But if you do it right, you'll get a whole lot more than candy and a remote control. You'll keep your job and make boatloads of actual dough!

IDENTIFYING SELECTS (A.K.A. SEEING STORY)

But how do we actually KNOW a "select" when we SEE it? What constitutes a select? Are there any rules or guidelines to follow?

Well, the honest answer is, THERE ARE NO RULES!

Pulling selects is the art of SEEING STORY. And in reality TV, story can come in ANY and ALL forms. Yes, you'll find obvious moments of essential action and dialogue. That's easy, but you also must find the less obvious INDIRECT moments that can be equally essential in building your story. Reality TV editing is about weaving a tapestry of separate, and sometimes unrelated, elements to make a scene that feels organic and REAL. It's about trial and error, mixing and matching, arranging and rearranging. So pulling selects all comes down to your gut instinct and common sense.

• • •

That said, a select can come in three basic TYPES: *Complete*, *Incomplete*, and *Out-of-Context*. Keeping them in mind as you work will help you separate the wheat from the chaff.

1. Complete Selects

These are the easiest and most obvious selects to identify. They are complete pieces of dialogue and transparent, easily understood moments of action that speak directly to the story you are trying to tell. They are strong sections of story that can be easily extracted from the raw and stand independently within your scene.

> ### *In the Bay:*
> Let's take our sample logline from the previous chapter: "GUY MEETS GAL IN CLUB AND GETS HER NUMBER."
>
> A **Complete Select** might be a shot of the woman getting a piece of paper from the bartender, writing down her number, and handing it to the guy. This is a clear and complete narrative moment that speaks directly to your plan. It needs only to be extracted from the raw and placed in the scene to serve its purpose.
>
> Another example might be the guy walking up to the gal, saying hello, and sitting next to her. Again, if this entire moment plays out in a clean and succinct fashion, if it can simply be lifted from the raw and placed in your edit without manipulation, it is a **Complete Select**.

2. Incomplete Selects

As clean and easy as complete selects can make the editor's job, they are by no means the trend in reality TV editing. (I wish it were that easy!) Most often you will deal with far smaller pieces—fragments of actions and dialogue called **Incomplete Selects**.

As I've said before, reality's raw footage is unpredictable. It is full of fruitless turns and tangents. These distractions often get in the way of the story you wish to tell. You may simply want to have Honey Boo Boo walk into the living room, sit down, and turn on the TV. But life is rarely as simple as we'd like it. Any number of things might have happened between the moment Honey stepped into the room and when she finally turned on that television. She might've grabbed the phone from her sister or started playing tug-of-war with the dog or spilled milk on herself or… They all might be interesting bits of story, but they're not YOUR story. You just need her to walk in, sit, and turn on TV. In order to achieve this, you will have to isolate those essential moments of story as incomplete selects, and assemble them later to make your scene.

In the Bay:

Let's take another look at our "Club" example to further illustrate **Incomplete Selects**.

Let's imagine that, in reality, our guy didn't just get her number in one clean shot. Instead, the raw footage plays out something like this:

She asks the bartender for a piece of paper. She and our guy continue talking while she waits. The bartender takes so long that she goes to the restroom and then comes back. They continue talking. Our guy receives and responds to a text. Finally, the piece of paper arrives and she starts to write her number, but the pen is out of ink. She asks a stranger for a pen. Then she and the stranger get into a conversation. While in that conversation, she writes her number down. But she still doesn't give it to our guy until after the stranger has left—a full 10 minutes later!

As you can see, there were numerous distractions and tangents surrounding the moments of story we need. We just want to see her a) take a piece of paper, b) write down her number, and c) give it to our guy. Maybe see a smile from him upon receiving it. That's all! Therefore, when pulling our selects we will have to extract each of these moments separately as incomplete selects or story fragments, and then assemble them later to make the complete moment we need.

3. Out-of-Context Selects

When pulling selects, you will often find that the actual reality captured by the camera does not progress as you'd like (does not clearly follow your scene's story) and/or does not give you all the material you need to make your scene. In these cases, you will be forced to use **Out-of-Context Selects**, which are moments of action or dialogue that did not happen at the same time or same place as your scene's main footage but are repurposed to fill in plot holes or otherwise suit the needs of the scene you're constructing.

Here's a little test for you. The next time you are watching *America's Next Top Model* and it cuts to a reaction shot of Tyra observing a model, ask yourself: *"Was this really the reaction Tyra was having at that moment? Furthermore, was this a reaction that even took place anywhere near that moment?"*

A large majority of the selects you pull will be out-of-context selects. They are (most often incomplete) pieces of story that are neither temporally nor organically connected to the moment you are building but, if positioned correctly, will seem as if they are.

In the Bay:

Let's take one more look at our "Club" scene to illustrate out-of-context selects.

Let's imagine that in the middle of our scene where the gal is giving the guy her number, the camera shuts off! We get up to the point where she begins to write, but that's it! That's where our footage ends. We have no shot of the guy looking over her shoulder as she writes, no shot of her handing the paper to the guy, and no shot of the guy smiling in satisfaction after he's received it.

What do we do? These are essential moments; the story doesn't work without them. Do we bag the scene? Is it game over?

What we do is look for our needed missing moments elsewhere in the raw footage. Let's look for shots that we can "cheat" (i.e., use out of context) to provide the moments the camera never caught.

Perhaps we find a completely unrelated shot from a completely different moment that shows the guy *looking over the gal's shoulder* as she shows him a picture on her iPhone. It has nothing to do with our story, but because it's a tight shot (too tight to see what the guy is actually looking at) and the guy is looking in the right direction, we can use it and no one will know the difference.

Next, let's say we find a shot of the gal handing her drink over to the guy so he can take a sip. If the drink is out of frame and all we really see is the gal *handing something to the guy*, why can't it be that piece of paper with her number on it? No reason why not.

Finally, let's say we have a *close-up of the guy smiling* after she has just complimented his eyes. Again, not at all related to the phone number, but if it's tight and nondescript enough, it can be taken out-of-context, pulled from the raw, and applied to our story to suit our purposes.

And there you have it: Three out-of-context selects have been repurposed to suit our needs, and a scene, once incomplete, is now whole.

Train yourself to see things out of context. This ability is at the core of all reality TV editing. It is the key to solving many of the problems and filling many of the holes left by the unpredictable and haphazard beast that is reality TV raw footage. Cheating and reorganizing reality is the name of the game, so learn it, love it, and practice, practice, practice it. More on this to come.

NOTE: All of the above information about selects not only applies to picture, it can also apply to sound, independent of picture. Sound is just as powerful an element and as useful a tool in crafting a story. So as you navigate your raw and pull your selects, be sure to keep your ears just as open as your eyes.

Organizing Your Selects

So, you have established your PLAN and given it a clear and succinct LOGLINE to keep you on track. And you know the various forms that selects come in. Now you are ready to step into a sea of disorganized raw footage and pull all the applicable selects needed to tell your story.

Okay, great, but where are you going to put all this stuff? Think like you're back in the grocery store. Your arms are full of ingredients. You need a cart to throw this stuff in!

There are numerous ways to organize material in a digital editing system. (I will explain more about what this system is and how it works in future chapters.) You can organize it by using locators, bins, clipboards, subclips, subsequences (again I will get into these terms with more detail later), etc. But the way I like to go is to put all of my material onto what is called a **Timeline**.

The Timeline:

I'm not going to get too technical here, but in video editing, a **Timeline** is the name given to the digital palette upon which you place and eventually edit your material. Think of it as a long, rectangular dining room table that you throw all of your crap on. You can move that crap around and organize it however you want. You can take stuff off or put more stuff on. You can stretch the table out to be as big as you want it to be, and you can squeeze it together to make it as small as you want.

On your computer, a **Timeline** would look something like this:

Here is an example of a blank timeline (nothing is on the table).

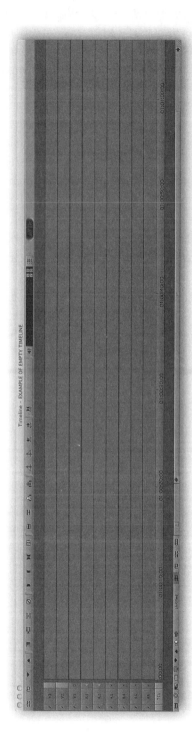

Here is an example of a timeline with clips (short or long moments of uninterrupted video or audio) placed on it. Each of these clips is a select pulled from raw footage.

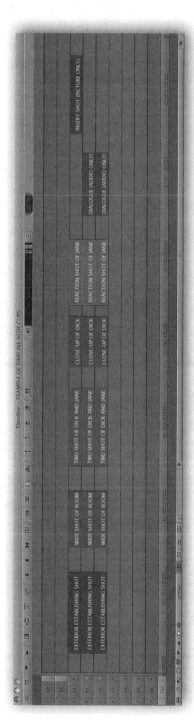

To gain a more detailed understanding of the timeline, I recommend you pick up an Avid or Final Cut Pro manual. You can also jump on the Web and do a little Wikipedia research on non-linear (a term we will define in future chapters) digital editing. Here's a link to get you started: http://en.wikipedia.org/wiki/Non-linear_editing_system.

A Little Chronology Never Hurts

One of the great things about the timeline onto which you're placing your selects is that you can shuffle stuff around on it any which way you please. And since you'll be using your selects to tell a story with a beginning, middle, and end, it might make sense for you to organize them CHRONOLOGICALLY—in the order you anticipate them appearing in your final edit.

Now this chronological organization doesn't need to be completely precise. Not every select has to be in exactly the right spot; you'll finesse that when you actually start editing. Still, the more you are able to place your selects on the timeline with some level of correct chronology, the easier it will be to find what you need, WHEN you need it. And here's a little secret: On a subconscious level, you will be starting to edit your scene without even knowing it. You will begin visualizing the story in your head as you encounter and organize the ingredients you will use to create it.

Take Note: The Producer Stringout

Sometimes producers will want to do your selects work for you. They will create a timeline of their own filled with all of the most memorable and/or story-appropriate moments from the raw. This is called the **Producer Stringout**. Personally, I tend to avoid these if I can.

The only occasion you may *need* to relent and work from a producer stringout is when time is working against you: If you have been given a tight, even unreasonable deadline that prohibits you from truly immersing yourself in the raw, then you may have no choice but to compromise and work solely from what has been selected for you. This is not ideal by any means, but it can happen and you need to be prepared for it.

I am not saying this to diminish the value of producers or their ability to recognize good content. Most of the producers that I have worked with over the years have been amazing. Much of what I know, I have learned from them.

The reason I discourage working from their stringouts is because they are not editors. They do not view footage the way editors do, so they do not pull selects the way editors do. There are far too many looks and nods, scraps of dialogue, and random cutaways (shots that may at first glance seem unimportant or off-topic, such as a shot of the bottles behind the bar in a bar scene, but which add color and depth to a scene) that can be missed by the untrained eye. A producer may pull all of the best story, but he or she may not pull all of the bits and pieces of raw necessary to fully construct that story.

Also, a funny thing happens as you navigate the raw and pull selects yourself; you get to know the footage. As you roll back again and again it begins to imprint itself on your subconscious mind. Little moments, even things you passed over initially, linger in your brain. I can't tell you how many times I've hit a wall in an edit and then remembered a random moment, a look, a laugh, or a cutaway from the raw that saved the day. I may not have pulled it, but I still remembered it because I DID THE PULLING. Raw footage is the clay from which you sculpt. You don't want to see just a portion of that clay; you want to be able to immerse yourself in all of it.

Right now you may be saying to yourself, "I thought if I had good field notes (see previous chapter) I didn't need to watch ALL of the raw." And that is true—to an extent. If you have days or tens of hours of raw footage, field notes will help you dial in on the sections pertinent to telling your story. They will keep you from wandering COMPLETELY astray and losing yourself in material that you will never use. But within the pertinent sections you should know all the footage thoroughly.

MARKING THE DEVIATIONS

Having a basic plan and using that plan to pull selects is essential to navigating the raw. It keeps you focused and protects you from the many twists, turns, and tangents that can throw you off track. But just because you have a focus and a plan doesn't mean that you should COMPLETELY disregard those twists, turns, and tangents. Some might be worth considering.

Within the heaps of raw footage there will often be moments of REALITY GOLD that are seemingly random and off track, but are still simply too good to completely ignore. Examples include:

- The terse business call that briefly interrupts Gene Simmons's romantic proposal scene.
- The kitchen fire that momentarily sidelines Tori and Dean's celebratory dinner scene.
- The celebrity spat that pops up during an *Apprentice* team's charity fund-raising scene.

These moments are what I call **Deviations**. They are the laughs, the tears, the fights, and the hookups that are unrelated to your plan, but can be *great* television. When I come across moments like these I mark them with a *locator* (an editing program's digital equivalent of a bookmark) so that I can return to them later and consider them further.

The process of building a scene can be unpredictable. Sometimes, despite your best efforts, your plan will backfire. Perhaps a technical mishap cannot be overcome or a missing plot point is just too great to circumvent. You never know when you will hit an insurmountable obstacle. By having these deviations tagged for future consideration, you allow yourself to return to the raw, quickly and efficiently consider "the best of the rest," and potentially try something new.

CLASSIC SELECTS FOR ALMOST ANY SCENE

Okay, you know the basics of PULLING SELECTS. You know what it is and how to go about it. And you know where to file your selects. Now, to sweeten this pot of knowledge, I'll list a few classic examples of shots that make for great selects in almost any scene. These are standard storytelling elements that are always useful to have at hand. They can often get you out of sticky situations.

The Reaction Shot

This is probably the most valuable out-of-context select to pull. Quite often the ACTUAL reaction that a character gives in a scene is less than ideal. A guy tells a joke but the gal doesn't laugh, or her laugh is half-assed. Even worse, the camera TOTALLY MISSED the laugh. The good news in this situation is that tight close-up reaction shots are pretty much interchangeable. Hank tells a joke. You cut to a CU (close-up) reaction shot of Kendra laughing. Was this laugh actually captured as a reaction to

Hank's joke, or was it captured twenty minutes earlier, in between takes, when the producer spilled a cup of coffee on his lap? IT DOESN'T MATTER. As long as the shot is tight enough (meaning that we won't notice background changes) and the eye-line works (meaning she's looking in the right direction), you can put that reaction shot anywhere you might need it in the scene.

Entrances and Exits

Shots in which a character enters or exits a scene are always useful, sometimes indispensable. There is no more literal way to visually say "We are entering a scene" or "We are leaving a scene" than with a clear **Entrance** or **Exit** shot. There are any number of scenarios where these shots may come in handy. They can be a great way to open a scene, reorient a viewer as you change locations, and even button (close) a scene that is lacking a clear and conclusive ending. I can't tell you here of all the ways entrances and exits can save your butt in an edit. But I can tell you that if you see them, pull them.

Dramatic and Emotional Outbursts

As a reality TV editor, a big part of your job is to make the most dramatic, energetic, and emotionally charged scene possible. Audiences tune in to see the laughing, the cheering, the screaming, and the crying. For this reason, if you happen upon a high-energy **Outburst** of any kind that could, in any way, work its way into your plan—PULL IT! Be liberal on this one. If a producer watches your cut and feels there's not enough energy in it, I guarantee he or she will ask for moments like this. And if that producer was in the field and actually SAW THAT MOMENT go down, or has studied the raw thoroughly enough to have noted it, you may be sure he is going to ask about it.

Exterior Establishing Shots

Generally, when a scene takes place inside any sort of structure (house, high-rise, business establishment, etc.), the production crew will shoot an **Exterior Establishing Shot** to help orient the viewer to the site. These establishing shots are always of value. They can be used to start a scene, end a scene, step away from a scene, reenter a scene, and even cover an awkward jump forward in the scene by suggesting the passage of time.

Signage

This is a variation on the establishing shot. Quite often when a scene takes place in a location that has some sort of **Signage** associated with it (a business sign out front, a city's "Welcome" sign, a park's entrance sign), the production crew will capture it. Once again, this is a great tool for orienting the viewer and establishing a scene. Also, in the case of businesses, in order to use a location the production crew often agrees to show its sign in the show as a form of advertisement. A producer will even sign contracts committing to this, so, once again, pull it.

Detail Shots

During a shoot, cameras often will move away from the scene's subjects and grab close-up **Detail Shots** of the environment. A detail shot might be generic, such as shot of a clock on the wall or some passing traffic. Or it might be a shot of a specific object that is referenced or regarded within the scene. In the case of our club scene, it might be a shot of the blank napkin sitting on the bar awaiting the woman's phone number. These shots can be put to use as valuable distractions. They can hide the abrupt and jarring visual jumps that sometimes arise from tightening or streamlining a scene's action. They can also reinforce key story points. The anticipation of our guy waiting for her number is only heightened when every time he looks down we can cut away to the blank napkin before him.

Body Shots

Just as the camera will move away from the subject to capture objects of interest, it will also close in on choice **Body Shots**, such as a clenching hand, or a nervously tapping foot. Sometimes, this sort of shot is used to reinforce or add depth to a particular action or dialogue exchange. Other times it is used simply to heighten an emotion or the level of tension in the scene. When positioned deftly within a cut, body shots can add insight into a character's emotional and psychological state. Again, just as with detail shots, these can also act as great cover-ups when streamlining and tightening the action of the scene.

Hellos and Goodbyes

Much like the aforementioned exits and entrances, **Hellos** and **Goodbyes** (onscreen characters greeting or taking leave of each other) are narrative conventions that any audience member can recognize. They are universal ways to say we are starting something (perhaps a new scene) or we are completing something, and when your scene lacks a clear start or finish, incorporating these moments can often save the day.

Traveling Shots

Scenes will not always take place in just one spot. Many times a character will move, changing position and even location. Now, this might be as simple as moving a few feet, but it can also be down the street, across town, or even across the Atlantic! Therefore, **Traveling Shots**, shots that suggest movement or travel from one place to another, are always good selects to pull. Such a select might be a character walking in front of the camera while crossing the street. Or, it might be a character's car driving past the camera as it makes its way down the freeway. Traveling shots help maintain a scene's orientation and continuity, while at the same time allowing you to jump quickly from one place to the next.

> ### In the Bay:
>
> Let's say you are editing a shopping scene for *Keeping Up with the Kardashians*. Kim is on a shopping spree and is painting the town with her credit card. She is bouncing from location to location, all around LA, and you need to smoothly incorporate this movement within a tight and simple scene.
>
> By adding a few choice shots of her walking down sidewalks, moving quickly past storefronts, and perhaps driving past the camera, you will be able to easily jump from store to store and purchase to purchase, without disorienting the audience or your scene.

Quick Head Turns

Technically, a **Quick Head Turn** is a reaction shot. That said, it is such a useful and valuable reaction shot that I felt it deserved to be singled out. Often when introducing a new and important dramatic element into a scene, you will want to call the audience's attention to it, and you will want to do this in the strongest way possible. Cutting to a quick head turn can do just the trick.

> ### In the Bay:
>
> I was recently cutting a stakeout scene in which a group of policemen were hiding out, waiting for a suspect. When the perp finally showed, I wanted the audience to feel the impact his appearance had on the cops. I wanted the audience to FEEL the cops' reaction, and I wanted to do so with a punch.
>
> How did I do it?
>
> As soon as the suspect rounded the corner, I cut to a **Quick Head Turn** coupled with a choice dramatic SFX (sound effect). There is no better way to say "HEY LOOK AT THAT!" or "THERE HE IS!" It's quick, easy, and requires no further explanation.

IT GETS EASIER

I know this whole PULLING SELECTS thing sounds like a tricky task. There are hours and hours of material to watch. How can you be sure to catch each and every crucial look, word, sound, and gesture as it passes by? Well, that's why you LOOK, LOOK, AND LOOK AGAIN! There's no such thing as one pass through the raw. You should make dozens of passes and learn the raw inside out. And, in time, as you progress in your job, you'll find that the more you practice, the keener your eye will get and the sharper your instincts will become.

When I was a child searching for sea glass, I had to know what I was looking for. I had to be able to discern green glass from seaweed and pink glass from a jellyfish. It was hard, intense work, and, yes, I made MANY a mistake. But a funny thing happened as I went along: The more I did it, the easier it became. At first I couldn't find a thing. I was frustrated and angry to see my smug sister plucking piece after precious piece while I floundered and steamed. But, as I trained myself HOW to look and exactly WHAT to look for, suddenly every pocket I had was overflowing with treasure! And my formerly gloating sister was suddenly not so cocky.

CHAPTER 2 REVIEW

Choose the correct answers from the lettered list.

1. What are the rules to know when pulling selects?

2. What are the three basic forms a select can come in?

3. ___ _____ is the "palette" upon which you place and eventually edit your material.

4. _____ are moments of REALITY GOLD that are seemingly random and off track, but still simply too good to completely ignore.

   a. The timeline
   b. Deviations
   c. There are no rules!
   d. Complete selects, incomplete selects, and out-of-context selects

Answers: 1-c, 2-d, 3-a, 4-b

CHAPTER 3

FROM SELECTS TO SCENE

I have lived in Southern California for more than a decade, and I can honestly say that I love it! What's not to love? The perfect weather, the amazing food, the beaches, the mountains, the desert...I can't imagine living anywhere else. But for all of its assets and advantages, it has one rather notable drawback: There is one price that every Angeleno must pay, one burden that we all must bear—TRAFFIC!

LA is known for having some of the worst bumper-to-bumper, accident-prone traffic in the United States. And as a driver in the thick of it, there is one crucial lesson to learn and learn quickly: *When planning a trip, the WHERE is absolutely useless without first knowing the HOW.*

In LA one should never hop in the car on a whim and just "go" somewhere. Knowing where you want to end up is not enough. There are often multiple ways to get to the same destination. And to blindly choose one route without considering all the others could spell disaster. There are just too many four-wheeled maniacs, confusing surface streets, and wildly unpredictable freeways. Choosing the wrong path could turn a fifteen-minute trip into a two-hour stress-fest! So before hopping into your car, it is essential to choose not just a path, but THE path.

How do you do this? Well, to effectively determine THE path, you must assess the many factors that might affect your journey: Is there construction? Is it rush hour? Where are the accidents? When do the schools let out? With these questions in mind, you must consider each possible route to your destination. Only then can you confidently resolve the most efficient way to get from point A to point B, with the fewest surprises.

How does this all relate to reality TV editing? Well, just as an LA driver must choose the right path to get through the chaos of cars, you too need to choose the correct path for navigating your way through your sea of footage.

Right now you have a basic story (your logline), and you have amassed a heavily laden timeline of selects. You know where you want to go, but you still don't know specifically HOW you're going to get there. So before you start editing, you need to assess your material and select the simplest, most efficient and streamlined route to telling your story.

TURNING YOUR *LOG*LINE INTO AN *OUT*LINE

Simply choosing this route, though, is not enough. Your selected raw footage can be a disorienting thing (even once it is laid out on a timeline). To keep yourself on track, you need to reference something physical. If you were driving somewhere, your reference would be a scrap of paper containing a list of directions. In reality TV editing, your reference is pretty much the same thing, but instead of listing the crucial lefts and rights of your drive, it lists the key twists and turns of your scene's story.

This list is called your **Outline**. And no reality edit should begin without one.

Finding Your Outline

Your outline represents the skeleton of your scene. It is a list of the essential steps necessary to get you from the beginning to the end of the story you want to tell. It turns your PLAN into a PLAN OF ATTACK.

To effectively find a scene's outline, keep two very important rules in mind: *Keep It Simple* and *Use the Best Stuff.*

1. **KEEP IT SIMPLE.** This rule is pretty self-explanatory. Remember, your scene is one of possibly dozens within the show. As such, brevity and concision are everything. Your job is to get in, serve your story, and get out. So, as you review your selects, always look for the strongest, most concise path available to tell your story. And draft an outline that reflects this path. What are the fewest, strongest, and most focused story points (your landmarks and left and right turns) you need to get the job done? What is essential and what is tangential? What is focused and what is divergent? Keep it clear and keep it moving from beginning to end.

2. **USE THE BEST STUFF.** The second rule is just as, or perhaps even more, important. Audiences tune into reality TV to see MORE than "reality." They tune in to see "HYPER-REALITY." You are first and foremost working in a medium of entertainment. Your audience wants to be ENTERTAINED: They want to be moved, tickled, frightened, and shocked. To do this well, you must present your story's BEST VERSION. So your job is to select not just the most concise and focused pieces of reality, but also the most entertaining (i.e., best) moments from among your selects. You need to judge each and every select as if you were the audience. What moves you? What makes you laugh, cringe, cry? What captures your interest and doesn't let go?

• • •

Your story needs clarity. It needs focus. But it also needs energy, personality, and color. As the editor, it is your job to construct an outline that balances all these elements.

Drafting the Outline

Okay, so we know what an outline is, what it should do, and what to consider when constructing it. Now let's make one. Let's put it on paper. And to do this, let's revisit our "Club Scene" from Chapter 1. Once again, here is our logline:

"GUY MEETS GAL IN CLUB AND GETS HER NUMBER."

Now let's imagine we've gone through the raw footage and pulled all of the selects we could find that relate to this story. We've reviewed these selects for clarity and focus as well as drama, emotion, and energy. And, after careful consideration, have decided on the PATH (as will be mapped in our outline) our story will take.

With that in mind, let's take our logline to the next level, turning it into an outline.

"GUY MEETS GAL IN CLUB AND GETS HER NUMBER"

BECOMES THE FOLLOWING OUTLINE:

1. A GUY WALKS INTO A CLUB
2. HE SEES A WOMAN SITTING ALONE AT THE BAR
3. HE APPROACHES HER AND INTRODUCES HIMSELF
4. HE BUYS HER A DRINK
5. HE CHARMS HER WITH A JOKE
7. HE GETS HER PHONE NUMBER
8. HE LEAVES

This is a basic outline, a story skeleton. This is the road map you will use to assemble your scene. Notice how simple, concise, and direct it is. Only the ESSENTIAL story points and actions are mentioned; there are no tangents and no excess. We get in and out quickly. Everything serves a purpose to get us from the scene's beginning to its end.

WHEN A PLAN COMES TOGETHER

We know the story we want to tell. We have a fully outlined plan of how to get there. So let's get going! It's time to start putting things together. It's time to make our first rough edit, or, as it's called in reality TV editing, our **ASSEMBLY**.

I've said it before and I promise I will say it again and again: Reality TV editing is all about trying things out. It's about mixing and matching and seeing what works. You are quite literally putting a puzzle together. Some pieces will be easy to place, but most will need to be placed, re-placed, positioned, repositioned, tweaked, trimmed, massaged, and intermingled. You want to tell your story with strength and clarity, and any number of selects might be the right combination to serve your plan. The only way to figure out which of these combinations is the VERY BEST is trial and error.

With this in mind, let's review three different types of selects and introduce a fourth type. Through their manipulation you will create your scene.

1. COMPLETE SELECTS. This is the easiest and most basic select. It is, simply put, a clear, complete piece of the story. It could be a concise line of dialogue, or perhaps a moment of direct, easily comprehended action.

> ### *In the Bay:*
>
> In our club example, a **complete select** might be:
>
> A shot of the guy walking up to the gal at the bar, introducing himself, and sitting down beside her. This would fulfill **outline step #3: HE APPROACHES HER AND INTRODUCES HIMSELF.**
>
> *or*
>
> A shot of our guy telling a joke, at which the gal laughs hysterically. This would fulfill **outline step #5: HE CHARMS HER WITH A JOKE.**
>
> These are clearly grasped and direct pieces of footage; they are complete story nuggets that fulfill the very simple demands of particular steps on our outline.

Complete selects should be the first pieces of your puzzle to be laid out. They will quickly give you a sense of what you have and what you need. Sometimes you will luck out and most, if not all, of the steps on your outline will be fulfilled by complete selects. Most of the time, though, completes will not fully fill out your scene, and you will have huge story gaps and narrative holes that will still need your attention.

2. INCOMPLETE SELECTS. When your footage allows you to tell your story in a set of simple, complete selects, you're in luck. You spot a shot of the guy introducing himself to the gal, or a shot of the guy charming her with a joke and you cut it in—mission accomplished! But, in reality TV editing, story can come in many different forms, and most of the time it comes in much smaller, INCOMPLETE pieces.

Incomplete Selects are story shards that must be combined with other story shards to create a greater whole.

> ### *In the Bay:*
>
> Let's say, within our pool of selects, we have isolated these four moments:
>
> A shot of our guy gesturing to the bartender.
>
> A shot of the bartender responding.
>
> A shot of a drink being handed over.
>
> A shot of money changing hands.
>
> Each of these moments is INCOMPLETE. By that I mean they are just fragments of what is needed to fulfill one of our outline steps. But combined (spliced into a sequence), they fulfill a crucial step in our outline—**step #4: HE BUYS HER A DRINK.**

3. OUT-OF-CONTEXT SELECTS. These selects—usually just very tiny story fragments—hold as much narrative value as any other selects, they just happen to have been shot at a time or place unrelated to the story moment at hand. But in the world of reality editing (as well as any and all film and video editing), what is and isn't RELATED lies in the eye of the beholder. If you can make a shot work, it really doesn't matter from whence it originated. I will expand on this idea further in the next chapter.

> ### In the Bay:
>
> Let's return to the four incomplete selects that make up our outline step #4:
>
> A shot of our guy gesturing to the bartender;
>
> A shot of the bartender responding;
>
> A shot of a drink being handed over;
>
> A shot of money changing hands.
>
> Let's say that these moments were captured at totally different times and have no direct relationship to one another. This means that the gesture to the bartender was unrelated to the bartender's response, which had nothing to do with the drinks being handed over, which had nothing to do with the money changing hands. Each of these moments is foreign to the others. When they are properly chosen and edited together, however, the audience will completely believe that these **out-of-context selects** depict a continuous bit of real-life activity.

4. INDIRECT SELECTS. This is an important new category of select. **Indirect Selects** are actions or pieces of clear, concise dialogue that may surround and support the steps of the outlined story you are trying to tell, but are not DIRECTLY tied to any of your outline's steps. (See examples of indirect selects in "In the Bay" below.) It's always a good idea to have a few indirect selects at hand to help you through your scene.

> ### In the Bay:
>
> Staying with our club example, perhaps the camera missed the moment when the woman actually gives the guy her number. But instead, you find a shot of him programming said number into his phone moments later. Put it in. See if it plays.

Or, perhaps the guy's exit from the club is clumsy or terribly low energy. But you do find a shot of him outside skipping down the street with glee. Try it out. Lose his exit, and after he bids the woman adieu, cut directly to the skipping shot. It wasn't specifically called for in your outline, but it serves the same purpose, and given the weakness of the actual exit, it is probably a much stronger way to end your scene.

Indirect selects should always be considered when building your ASSEMBLY because, if the directly related footage you need for a step doesn't exist, indirect footage can save the day and rescue your plan.

Take Note: The Radio Cut

Building your first ASSEMBLY can be a messy business. And this is never more certain than when it comes to VISUAL CONTINUITY. Rearranging and streamlining content will no doubt leave you with many jarring continuity jumps. From shot to shot, people might change position, action, even demeanor.

Let's say you are dealing with a wedding toast given by Rob Kardashian at his sister Kim's wedding. The toast goes on forever and most of it is pretty boring. You decide to trim the toast down. You want to cut from the beginning of the toast to a few choice lines in the middle and then right to his finish. The problem is that the entire thing was shot in one uninterrupted close-up, so once you trim it up and pull the pieces together, you're left with a bunch of visual hiccups.

These picture bumps may be hidden in any number of ways, many of which we will discuss later in this book. BUT, when you are first starting out, when you are putting your SELECTS together for the first time, when you are building your initial ASSEMBLY, it is helpful to follow one very simple rule: FORGET YOUR EYES AND USE YOUR EARS.

You are assembling your story, not polishing it. You are testing different footage combinations, mixing and matching, and seeing what works and gets your story across. If you bog yourself down trying to smooth every visual hiccup you see, you are going to impede your progress.

So, instead of WATCHING the flow of your early cuts, LISTEN to it. Close your eyes, press PLAY, and see if Rob's streamlined toast flows. Does it still make sense? Do you buy it? Would you believe that this new condensed version WAS the speech he ACTUALLY gave? This is called building a **radio cut**. You are assembling the audio of your story first and massaging the video later.

The **radio cut** can be an invaluable tool when building your first ASSEM-BLY. Remember, as you work toward your final scene edit, you will be taking parts away, adding them back, moving them this way and that. You need the flexibility, the freedom, and most importantly, the TIME to do so. You can't afford to get bogged down in picture bumps and continuity jumps. You need to focus on building the strongest story first and making it pretty later.

WHEN A PLAN *DOESN'T* COME TOGETHER

Okay, to review. We have our OUTLINE. We know the different types of SELECTS we have at our disposal. We have chosen a body of various selects to build with. And we have begun the process of combining these selects to construct our first ASSEMBLY.

But this is just the beginning of the editing process. No matter how many selects you try, chances are you will still need more. Rarely does raw footage provide absolutely EVERY last thing you need. This is unscripted real life. There will almost always be holes in the captured footage. There will be moments and shots that you just don't have. There will be spoken lines and reaction shots that simply do not exist. The camera was pointed in the wrong direction. The sound guy didn't get the line. The energy sucked. The shot was out of focus. Whatever the case, there will most assuredly be crucial elements missing. There will be gaping chasms with nothing to fill them, and it will be up to YOU to find a solution.

Wait, WHAT? How do you "find a solution" for something that's not there? How do you fill a gaping hole with something that does not exist?

Well, this is where things really get interesting!

CHAPTER 3 REVIEW

Choose the correct answers from the lettered list.

1. Listing the key twists and turns of your story. Writing out its "directions." This is called making _____. And no reality edit should begin without one.

2. What are the two rules to keep in mind when constructing an effective outline?

3. In reality TV editing, what is your first rough edit called?

4. When building your first rough edit, what are the different types of elements you will be manipulating to make your scene?

5. By making a _____ _____ you are assembling the audio of your story first and massaging the video later.

    a. An assembly
    b. Outline
    c. Radio cut
    d. Complete selects, incomplete selects, out-of-context selects, indirect selects
    e. Keep it simple and use the best stuff

Answers: 1-b, 2-e, 3-a, 4-d, 5-c

WATCH AND LEARN

The very first "watch and learn" exercise in Chapter 1 challenged you to watch an episode of your favorite reality show and generate a **logline** for each and every scene. I'd like you to revisit that list and that same show now. I want you to re-watch the show and, as you do, try to take each **logline** a step further and turn it into an **outline**. I want you to identify the essential steps that bring you from the beginning to the end of each scene. Remember, you only want those steps that are most fundamental. You are trying to imagine the skeleton, the backbone, and the throughline of the scene.

CHAPTER 4

THE ART OF THE CHEAT

"It's funny, reality TV has this sort of f'd-up integrity. Sure we cheat footage. Sure we exaggerate emotions. Sure we manipulate things to focus the story. But it's still, on some level, real life. It's a kind of honest dishonesty."

Jackson Anderer, Editor,
Extreme Makeover: Home Edition and *Celebrity Apprentice*

I am a huge movie buff; actually, calling me a fanatic would probably be more accurate. And of all the incredible films and filmmakers that I've gobbled up over the years, perhaps my favorite is the late American auteur Stanley Kubrick. For me, there is no more brilliant and enigmatic filmmaker. His films are at once arresting and utterly original. Just think about it. Can you believe the same filmmaker behind *2001: A Space Odyssey* also made *Dr. Strangelove* AND *Barry Lyndon*?

Over the years I've made it my mission to soak up every interview, biography, and documentary available on the man. There isn't much, and what does exist is often less than revealing. But there is one resource that does deliver—one document that, in my opinion, digs deeper than any other. And that is the short documentary film that Kubrick's daughter made during the filming of *The Shining*.

Never before had anyone been afforded such intimate access to the reclusive man and his elusive process. The documentary includes out-takes from *The Shining*, behind-the-scenes discussions with Kubrick, and candid interviews with its stars. It is chock-full of incredible filmmaking insights and Kubrickian revelations. One interview, or to be more precise, one sentiment from one interview in particular truly struck me. It was conducted with the star of the film, Jack Nicholson, who discusses his struggles with trying to nail what would arguably become one of his most enduring performances. He talks about his intense desire to *"get this thing real,"*—to truly reflect how his character would *actually* behave. He says that he went mad with *realism* until a simple challenge from Kubrick changed his world. Kubrick said to him (and I'm paraphrasing): *"Sure it's real. But is it interesting?"*

Can you imagine how forgettable the character of Jack Torrance would be if Nicholson just went with REAL? The reason his performance as that character is so timeless is because Nicholson was unhinged in a larger-than-life way. It's because he was free to be so deliciously over-the-top (i.e., UNREAL). To me, Kubrick's point was dead on. People don't escape into entertainment; they don't lose themselves in fantasy just to see something REAL. REAL can get REAL boring REAL quickly. We have more than our fair share of REAL in REAL life. This is why good reality television, the kind that people can't get enough of and tune into again and again, is so much *more* than REAL.

Reality TV editing is all about FAKING IT. It's all about THE CHEAT. Reality may be based on real life, but it's still TV, and this is still HOLLYWOOD. On a show like *Jersey Shore*, chances are that many of the fights, hookups, and benders are not exactly what they seem to be. Such productions are a combination of what actually happened, what the producer faked on set, and what the editor cheated in post. Reality shows are NOT documentaries; they may contain honest moments of true experience, but that is just one ingredient in the dish. In truth, reality TV shows are carefully CONSTRUCTED objects of entertainment. They are fantasy, and if you've done your editing job correctly, viewers will embrace that fantasy and lose themselves in it with glee. If you haven't, they will simply change the channel.

IF YOU CAN'T BEAT IT, CHEAT IT

The reality TV editor's "License to Cheat" can infuse a show with color, energy, and edge. It can make the REAL into the UNREAL (and vice versa). It can also be a lifesaver when it comes to the many roadblocks and obstacles of dealing with reality's raw footage. At the end of the last chapter I talked about how raw footage never DIRECTLY gives you everything you need to tell your story. You'll never have every important line in close-up, nor will you have every action and reaction you need, at your fingertips. You will not simply find all of the elements you need to fulfill your plan, piece them together, and call it a show. It just doesn't work that way. Some of the elements will exist, certainly, and that's what we sift out and put aside when pulling selects. The rest, though, you will need to fabricate—which is to say CHEAT. We all know the old saying *"Necessity is the mother of invention."* Well, in reality TV, *"LACK OF FOOTAGE is the mother of invention!"* I will expand on this with more detail in a moment, but first I want to discuss a larger concept that is essential to the art of the cheat.

Your raw footage can be used in countless ways to cheat reality. But in order to even begin to imagine them, we first need to discuss a most important concept —**NON-LINEAR EDITING**.

LINEAR VS. NON-LINEAR

When I first started my training to be an editor I worked with a *linear* video editing system. I had two VHS video decks and a device that allowed me to control them. One deck was for playing my source shots and the other one was for recording my edited video as it was "cut" ("compiled" would perhaps be a more accurate term) together. When working with this system, I had to cut in chronological—i.e., linear—order, shot by shot. And to get from one source shot to another, I had to fast-forward through lots of unwanted footage. On the machine I recorded to, there were NO fast or easy re-dos. Once I cut in a shot, there was no altering the edit without starting the process over from scratch.

In the editing world, a linear system is one that cannot be accessed by hopping about at will. To get to, let's say, point E from point A, one must go past points B, C, and D, in that order. In the old days (not so very long ago), this did not seem inconvenient because reel-to-reel and cassette audio tapes and VHS and Beta video cassettes were all linear mediums—and they were the common video and audio storage mediums for both the professional and the man in the street.

In Ye Olde Linear Bay:

If I were editing the "Club Scene" from Chapter 1 with a LINEAR system:

I would first cut in the shot of the guy entering the club. Then I would cut in the CU of his face scanning the club. Then I would cut in the POV shot of the woman sitting alone at the bar, and so on.

If I made a mistake, or if I later came across a better entrance or line delivery, it would be too late. In order to use the better shot I'd have to start from the beginning again and re-edit everything. LINEAR suggests a straightforward order.

Reality editing is anything but.

Webster's Dictionary defines "non-linear" as: "Other than, not of, relating to, or resembling a straight line." What does this mean to us, as aspiring editors? It means that on a non-linear system we can hop about from one video or audio moment to another at will. If we want to go to moment E from moment A, we can simply, and almost instantaneously, do so—without passing through moments B, C, and D.

Both the professional and the man in the street have been living in an increasingly non-linear world for many years. A computer's hard drive is a non-linear system, as is an iPod and a DVD player and a CD player and hundreds of other everyday devices. So, it's not hard to get one's head around the non-linear concept—it's part of our daily lives.

With the introduction of NON-LINEAR video editing in the mid-1990s, the craft of assembling a video story was revolutionized: Footage was digitized and stored in computer memory. So altering the sequence and length of events was easily and quickly accomplished. Moving from moment B to moment Z took only nanoseconds! On a non-linear editing system, all your material is equally easily and immediately accessible ("random access" is the tech term for this).

On a NON-LINEAR editing system, any shot you might want is available to you almost instantaneously and can be moved, extended, trimmed, reversed, and inverted any which way, again and again, by simply tapping a few computer keyboard keys. You can move at any time to any part of your edit in a split second and alter whatever you please. If you find a better entrance for your "Club Scene," you can jump right to that spot in your edit and make the swap. Everything else remains unchanged, and can automatically snug up to your new footage, even if it is of a new length. You want to make a shot longer? Shorter? You want to see what the end would look like at the beginning or vice versa? You can do it.

Editing has always been about manipulating your elements, but when the computer-based Avid Media Composer and Final Cut Pro editing systems became the standards of the industry, the potential for manipulation and alteration video footage was multiplied 1,000 times over. And this is a good thing—because in reality TV editing, manipulation is the name of the game.

BREAK IT DOWN!

In order to fully harness the power and potential of non-linear video editing, you must first learn to BREAK IT DOWN: You must train yourself to see and hear the things you work with at their most elemental level. Any and every picture moment and any and every sound moment can be broken down, pulled out, and separated from that which surrounds it. Audio and video should ALWAYS, ALWAYS, ALWAYS be considered two VERY SEPARATE ELEMENTS.

In the Bay:

Just because you have a shot of reality star JWOWW looking at the camera and saying, *"Hi there,"* doesn't mean that you should only see and use that moment in just that way. For example, you might want to split the "Hi" and the "there" from one another and use them independently.

Let's say you have a scene where reality star Snooki asks JWOWW, "Where's the Jim Beam?" But unfortunately the camera operator turned the camera off before capturing JWOWW's response. You could take your close-up "Hi there," lose the "Hi," and now you have the response the camera missed:

"Where's the Jim Beam?"

"There."

The context of JWOWW's line has been completely changed. The use of the word "there" initially had nothing to do with bourbon, but now it does.

A problem has been solved and the viewer is none the wiser. This manipulation, this construction, is a perfect example of breaking down your elements and CHEATING your footage.

Train yourself to BREAK IT DOWN: Learn to see every moment of every video and audio element at its most elemental level. Allow yourself to see the timeline before you as an ever-changing organism where things can be broken apart, moved around, and intermingled however you please. If you do, a scene's obstacles, plot holes, and missing moments will become easy fixes, as opposed to deal breakers and story killers.

WHAT ORDER?

As I've stressed, one of the great benefits of non-linear editing is that you can mix, match, and move shots, sections, and scenes any which way you wish. As such, chronology—the order in which a thing happens—is completely flexible. And when it comes to reality TV editing, CHEATING THE ORDER of events can have a huge impact on your scene.

- Just because, in reality, an *Amazing Race*r gets stuck in traffic halfway through the race doesn't mean that you can't move that obstacle down to the final intense moments before he reaches the finish line.
- Just because a *Hell's Kitchen* competitor set fire to the oven several hours AFTER he caught Chef Ramsey's fury, doesn't mean that those two moments (the chef's wrath and the oven fire) can't be flip-flopped so that the fire appears to be the impetus for Ramsey's anger.

Cheating the order of events can often heighten drama (as my examples above demonstrate), fill gaps in logic, and provide a character's motivation where it might not otherwise exist. Time and chronology are as malleable as anything else in the non-linear world, and the ability to see and act on this can make a big difference in the fight to turn raw video into a focused, dramatic, and meaningful story.

CHEATING ON THE JOB

I recently ran into a problem while trying to edit a scene that depicted a rather juicy moment between a competitor and the show's host. Midscene, while the show's host explained the game's rules, the competitor suddenly, and without warning, became dizzy and fainted! It was an incredibly dramatic turn of events, and easily the highlight of the show. The only problem was that as soon as the competitor fell to the floor the crew shut off their cameras, and when the cameras were turned back on, he was up, composed, and ready to continue the challenge. The moments where he gets up, is comforted by the host, and regains his strength were completely missing. Without these story beats the scene's progression would make no sense. How can he be on the floor, passed out one minute, and then up, fully recovered, and back to it the next?

My boss, the show's executive producer, told me that if I couldn't find a solution I was to cut the faint. CUT THE FAINT? I wasn't about to do that. This was easily the best moment in the show. I couldn't imagine losing it. But the executive producer IS the executive producer. If I couldn't make the faint work, I would have no choice. It was on my shoulders. A key moment of reality gold would live or die based on what I could come up with. So what did I do?

THE STEPS TO MY SOLUTION:

    1. REVERSE THE FALL

    2. HIDE A MOUTH

    3. FAKE SOME CONCERNED DIALOGUE

    4. CHEAT A REASSURING RESPONSE

Cheat #1: Reverse the Fall

The first thing I did was reverse the shot of the faint. When I say "reverse" I mean I literally made it play backwards. So now, instead of dizzily FALLING to the ground, it would look as if the man was dizzily RISING to his feet (luckily the action had been captured by two cameras simultaneously, and by cutting between their two angles I was able to disguise the fact that we were literally seeing the same exact action played backwards). Underneath these reversed shots I put any heavy breathing, grunting, and groaning I could find to suggest that the man was struggling to get himself up.

Cheat #2: Hide a Mouth

Next I found a "two shot" (a wide shot showing two people) of the host and the contestant from moments before the faint. Our character is standing and listening to the host. Since this was just moments before the faint, our character already looked flushed and woozy—just the look I needed.

And, best of all, I found an extended section in the two-shot where the host is turned away from the camera so that his face and mouth are completely hidden from the audience. MOMENTS LIKE THIS ARE WORTH THEIR WEIGHT IN CHEATING GOLD! Having any shot in which a character is talking but his mouth is hidden from view means that he can now—through the magic of cheating the audio track—say anything you want. You can put any number of questions, confessions, revelations, or proclamations in this character's voice beneath this shot and the audience will buy it hook, line, and sinker!

Cheat #3: Fake Some Concerned Dialogue

My next step was to do just this, give the host something new to say. I began to scour days of raw footage looking for any time the host said anything that might work to solve my problem. I was able to find three separate OUT-OF-CONTEXT fragments of dialogue that fit the bill.

One was a moment from earlier in the week when the host told another cast member to "Take it easy!" because she was getting out of hand. The next was a moment when the camera was rolling between scenes and the host told an off-screen producer, "It's okay," in response to a technical question. The last audio fragment was a moment just before the man had fainted when the host had asked him, "Are you all right?" Even though I had used this piece of dialogue in scene already, I decided to use it again here, as it seemed like something the host might ask again in a situation like this.

I pulled only the audio portions of these three moments, and edited them together. (Remember, always recognize and judge audio and video as separate elements.) I then placed them beneath my two-shot. Now the host is heard saying, *"Take it easy. It's okay. Are you all right?"* And, because his face and mouth are hidden, it really APPEARS as though that's what he's saying IN THAT MOMENT. He now seems to be attending to our ailing man, who APPEARS to have just "lifted himself," grunting and groaning, from the floor.

Cheat #4: Cheat a Reassuring Response

The last piece of the puzzle was easy. I simply scoured all of the tight close-up shots of our fainting man from both before and after the faint until I found a clear and concise, albeit OUT-OF-CONTEXT, affirmative nod. Who or what he was actually nodding to made no difference. It was a tight close-up and it cut perfectly. I buttoned the scene with said nod and suddenly I had the recovery scene my boss demanded!

Now, the man pulls himself to his feet, grunting and groaning. The host turns to him in a two-shot and says, *"Take it easy. It's okay. Are you all right?"* Finally, in close-up, the man nods in the affirmative and the scene continues.

> *"A great way to hone your cheating skills is by editing single-camera scenes, meaning scenes shot with just one camera. You must consider all of your footage to make a scene work, and as your material narrows, the more creative you are forced become."*
>
> Anthony Rivard, Editor,
> *Top Chef* and *The X Factor*

A Few More Examples of Cheating

THE SURPRISE PARTY: A birthday-girl enters a dark room just as the lights flash on and her friends yell, "Surprise!" The problem? Her reaction is lame. Her energy is low and she honestly doesn't even appear surprised. Remember, this is real life. You can't script this girl's reaction. And you can't do a take two. What you get is what you get—or is it?

What can we do? How do we solve this? Well, let's imagine we scan the raw and find that, thirty minutes later, while opening her gifts, she actually IS surprised, she actually HAS energy, and she actually EXPRESSES enthusiasm. Break it down. Take the audio from this "gift" section and cheat it earlier.

Now she enters the room, the lights flash on, her friends yell, "Surprise!" and every time we cut away from her face to a reaction shot of the gathered celebrants we sneak in one of her high energy "gift" lines: ***"Oh My Gosh!" "No you didn't!" "You Guys!"*** Her face alone did not sell excitement, but coupled with these off-screen cheats, we are able to make it work. Suddenly we've upped the energy of her entrance 100-fold. And all by breaking it down, considering each element separately, and cutting together what we needed to improve the scene.

THE JUDGMENTAL DESIGNERS: We are cutting a dress prep scene for *Project Runway*. The scene needs to focus on Jerome, the laziest and most obnoxious designer of the bunch. We are to show him carelessly and sloppily assembling his garment while other designers watch and judge from across the room. We have great interview bites from the others condemning Jerome and his careless demeanor, and this is all building toward a scene to come where the entire cast will turn on Jerome and push for his elimination

The problem? When we dive into the raw we discover that there are NO looks from the fellow designers. There are no pursed mouths, shaking heads, or eye rolls. The other designers were so focused on getting their OWN work done, they didn't have time to watch and judge their careless competitor. So what do we do? We have all these great interview bites and no looks to tee them up. How can we make this scene play without such a crucial piece of the puzzle? Well, we look for a cheat.

Let's say, as we are scouring the raw, we discover that a few minutes before the competition began, while everyone was waiting around, Jerome took a call from his boyfriend. What started out as a chat quickly turned into a loud and obnoxious phone spat. It was so annoying that Jerome's fellow competitors couldn't help but steal judgmental glances and roll their eyes in disdain. There you have it. These glances, no matter how out of context, are just the cheats you need. Provided they are close-up enough, with relatively nondescript backgrounds, simply intercut them with the shots you can find of Jerome lazily assembling his garment. Now they are not judging his conversation, they are judging his work. You have found the material to tee up your sound bites and deliver the story of your scene.

FINAL WORDS ON CHEATING

Have you ever marveled at great magicians? They hold a certain power over their audience. They possess a gift that can make even the most skeptical of critics fall at their feet. An editor's great reality cheat is much like a great magic trick. It is quite literally making the impossible into the possible. And if you do it right, you can inspire the same awe from YOUR audience—and your employer.

The more you practice CHEATING, and the more sensitive you become to the many opportunities for invention that lurk within the raw, the more valuable you will become in the workplace. You will easily solve story and coverage problems that a lesser editor cannot. And great editing is nothing if not the ability to solve even the toughest of problems quickly and effortlessly. Too many editors will throw up their hands and claim there is no solution. They are the ones who don't get hired back, don't get raises, and don't get the pick of the litter when it comes to projects. The more solutions you can find and manipulate from the raw, and the more rabbits you can pull out of your editorial hat, the longer, healthier, and more lucrative your career will be!

CHAPTER 4 REVIEW

Choose the correct answers from the lettered list.

1. If you can't beat it, _____ it!

2. In _____ video editing, media can be moved, extended, trimmed, reversed, and inverted any which way again and again.

3. In order to fully harness the power and potential of non-linear video editing, you must first learn to what?

4. Audio and video, should ALWAYS, ALWAYS, ALWAYS be considered what?

5. One of the great benefits of non-linear editing is that you can alter the _____ in which things happen.

    a. Non-linear
    b. Break it down
    c. Cheat
    d. Order
    e. Separate elements

Answers: 1-c, 2-a, 3-b, 4-e, 5-d

WATCH AND LEARN

Go grab a recorded episode of your favorite competition reality show, a piece of paper, and a pen. Try to pick a big one such as *Survivor* or *Big Brother*. Now I want you to find the biggest competition scene you can within the show. (Hint: It's generally towards the end.) Once you find it, watch it through. As you do, write down any shot or moment that you think might possibly be a **cheat**. Are you hearing dialogue while not seeing the mouth from which it is supposedly originating? Do you suspect that the order of certain events may have been altered for dramatic effect? Could a particular character's reaction shot have been taken out of context and repositioned to heighten the scene? Use your imagination. Challenge yourself to identify every shot or fragment or sound that might possibly have been manipulated. There may be no way of knowing for sure what is a cheat and what is not, but by imagining what MIGHT be a cheat you will be on your way to reorienting the way you see and hear.

CHAPTER 5

KNOW YOUR BITES

It's funny how in life there are certain things you just cannot do. There are certain gifts you just are not born with. Personally, I am terrible at sports, I have a horrible singing voice, and when I "dance" people tend to turn UP the lights and turn OFF the music. However, just as we have deficits that can trip us up and hold us down, we also have ASSETS or advantages that can give us a big leg up. We each have our own special strengths, our own secret weapons, and our own gifts that, if used correctly, can put us ahead of the rest in the game of life.

Reality TV editing has its deficits too. Raw footage is often random-seeming and full of roadblocks: A good story can be elusive. The footage's production value can be nonexistent. And a viable sense of continuity (one moment appearing to belong to the next moment, or at least appearing to have come from the same planet) can be nearly impossible. But, it also has its strengths. There are certain assets and secret weapons that reality TV enjoys and employs that other forms of television cannot. Perhaps the most powerful of these is THE INTERVIEW.

> *"The freedom and latitude we as editors are allowed when employing the interview within our work makes reality TV different from every other type of storytelling."*
>
> Ali Grossman, Editor,
> *The Real Housewives of New York* and *Extreme Makeover: Home Edition*

Most reality television shows use interviews with their characters/ participants to help tell and/or accentuate the stories these shows want to tell. Usually such interviews are broken down into smaller pieces—known as *bites* (as in "sound bites": short recorded bits of audio)—and employed wherever needed throughout a show. These interviews might be captured during the production, or directly following it, or even weeks after the fact. They might be shot in a formal "sit down" style or captured raw, hand-held and on-the-fly.

But no matter when or how they are captured, interview bites are invaluable pieces of the reality TV puzzle. An interview bite is often the saving grace, the missing link, and the life raft that keeps an otherwise sinking scene afloat. Therefore, it is essential that you have a strong understanding of the shapes this powerful device can take, and the ways it can be used and ABUSED within a cut.

TYPES OF INTERVIEW

When you are building your scene plan and assembling your edit you will often find yourself in need of an interview bite. There might be a hole in your scene's logic or continuity or flow that you cannot fill, a moment that needs clarification, or an emotion that needs reinforcement. Whatever the case, it is your job to locate and insert that bite into your cut.

Sounds simple right? Not so much. Before you can cut a bite into a scene, you first need to know what KIND of bite the scene demands. So, before we can discuss the many uses for and benefits of the interview bite, we first need to understand the different forms it can take. Like most things in reality TV, classification can be difficult, so to keep things simple I have turned to the sports world for two essential categories that any and all interview bites can fit into. They are **PLAY-BY-PLAY** and **COLOR COMMENTARY**.

Play-by-Play

Just as in sports, a **Play-by-Play** bite is a piece of interview that reports factual information. It recounts story, delivers stats (a.k.a. character details), and provides viewers with all sorts of objective data that they might need to know.

Below are a few examples of play-by-play bites:

- **"My name is Scott Baio. I'm 49 years old and single."**
- **"When I got back to the *Big Brother* house it was completely trashed. There was garbage everywhere and nobody in sight."**
- **"It's Sunday, and I'm taking John and Jennifer to my favorite bakery to sample wedding cakes."**

Each of these examples expresses objective information that informs the viewer of fact-based story details (the *play-by-play*).

Such a bite can be a huge asset, and in some instances a "plan saver." But it MUST be used sparingly. A little goes a long way with play-by-play.

If you are dealing with an important story beat, the actual reality of the moment is ALMOST ALWAYS much more engaging, emotive, and memorable than any interviewee's recollection of the event. Viewers want to experience the moment as it happens, not hear about it after the fact. Still, if used correctly, a snippet of play-by-play can be a powerful and effective storytelling device. It can focus the plot and keep the story from straying. It can heighten stakes by providing important backstory and personal details, and it can clarify confusion, keeping the audience up to speed every step of the way.

Color Commentary

The most encompassing classification for the interview bite is **Color Commentary**. This type of bite is not meant to recount the story or fill in essential facts. Instead, it is meant to heighten, accentuate, and COLOR the story by adding new dimension to it.

Color commentary bites deal less with the objective or factual and more with the *subjective*—opinions, feelings, emotions. You might color events with someone's opinion. You might shape a character by revealing his or her emotional state. You might heighten the tone and add energy to a scene with an expressive high-energy outburst. Color commentary can often *humanize* what the viewer sees on the screen. It can also infuse a scene with the energy necessary to turn it from average to extraordinary.

Below are a few examples of color commentary bites:

- **"I hate Snooki. She is such a loudmouth. I think she should be kicked out of the house."**

- **"Right now I'm really terrified. What if I freeze up? What if I crack? What if Chef Ramsey hates me?"**

- **"PLEASE! Tyra is such a sucker. I've got this competition in the bag!"**

Each of these examples is completely subjective. There is no narrating or factual recounting here. These are bites that express opinion, perspective, emotion, and personality.

The color commentary bite is an essential ingredient in the reality TV mix. If chosen correctly and inserted wisely, a choice bit of color commentary can infuse a scene with tension, drama, humor, fear, and any number of other exciting states or temperaments I can't think of right now.

• • •

Now that we have a handle on the two major categories of interview bites, let's look at some of the more common ways that a choice bite can benefit your scene.

NARRATIVE USES FOR THE INTERVIEW

"I think a bite works best when it adds new dimension to a scene. It's about injecting another layer of emotion or perspective. It's about adding subtext to the scene. Those are the kinds of bites I like to use."

Tim Roche, Editor,
It's Always Sunny in Philadelphia and *Undercover Boss*

A strong understanding for the many NARRATIVE ways that interview bites can be used is essential to harnessing their power.

The Perspective Bite (Color Commentary)

This is a bite that can allow us to step into a character's mind, to see events through that character's eyes. Our opinions are thus influenced and directed by the character's opinions.

A reality show's footage is captured by a camera operator, whose job it is to remain objective, to simply cover the moments in the most technically proficient manner. **Perspective bites**, however, allow us to transcend this objectivity. They can help us humanize the scene by coloring it with a unique and personal focus.

EXAMPLE:

    A cop approaches a drunken man on the street and says
    "Hello." The drunk takes one look at him and starts
    laughing.

```
CUT TO A PERSPECTIVE BITE FROM OUR COP:
                    COP
This situation is just crazy! Not only is
this guy a complete loon, he's so drunk he
could get you wasted with a sneeze!
```

In this instance, the details of the event alone are actually somewhat mild. A cop walked up and said hello. A drunk started laughing. Big whoop! But by adding the cop's view of the events through a perspective bite, they suddenly take on a much larger and more dramatic tone. He is giving us his opinion and thus helping to shape our own. What was initially a drunken man laughing at a cop is now a VERY DRUNKEN MAN and a COMPLETE LOON in a CRAZY situation. Suddenly the character becomes much more colorful, and the cop's actions and dialogue take on a much more focused emotional reality. Now every time the cop speaks, we know in his mind he's talking, not just to a drunken man, but to a WASTED CRAZY PERSON!

The Emotional State Bite (Color Commentary)

This is possibly the most commonly used type of interview bite in reality TV, and for good reason. Whether your character is happy, sad, angry, or terrified, an **emotional state bite** is one of the most dramatic and effective ways to help define a moment for the viewer.

While a **perspective bite** is focused outward, the **emotional state bite** is firmly focused inward. It's all about what and how a person is feeling emotionally in the moment. It is one thing for a character to express their REASON for competing on *The Amazing Race*. It is another for them to tell the audience how it makes them FEEL. *"I am terrified I won't finish this race. I would be mortified if I went home a loser!"* We are emotional animals. This is how we relate to and connect with the world. To gain insight into what a character is FEELING is to get the closest you can to experiencing the moment firsthand.

EXAMPLE:

```
A cop approaches a drunken man on the street and says
"Hello." The drunk takes one look at him and starts
laughing.

CUT TO AN EMOTIONAL STATE BITE FROM OUR COP SAYING WITH
A GRIMACE:
```

> COP
> **This just pisses me off! My blood is boiling right now. I am livid. I don't care how drunk you are, you don't disrespect the uniform!**

We all know what it is to be livid. We can look within ourselves, revisit our own emotional past, and find that feeling. By applying this emotional state to the character, the scene becomes charged with subtext. The Cop is no longer just a cop. He is a blood-boiling, livid cop who is doing everything in his power to maintain composure. He is a human being. He is one of us. It is now much easier to step into his shoes and truly live the experience of the story.

The Personality Bite (Color Commentary)

The **personality bite** is probably the hardest to define as it can come in many shapes and sizes. In general, though, it is an abrupt, off the cuff, often humorous remark intended to infuse a scene and a character with PERSONALITY! It is very much a stylistic touch and is often found in lighter, more tongue-in-cheek shows.

EXAMPLE:

A cop approaches a drunken man on the street and says "Hello." The drunk takes one look at him and starts laughing.

CUT TO A PERSONALITY BITE FROM OUR COP SAYING WITH A SMIRK:

> COP
> **I don't know what's so funny. Maybe I should have some of what he's having!!!**

or

> COP
> **Was it something I said???**

or

> COP
> **Don't you just love Saturday nights???**

or

> COP
> **"Oh boy, here we go!!!"**

This is not exactly an opinion or perspective, although we can pretty easily deduce his opinion of the drunk and the situation. Instead, this is simply a colorful remark intended to showcase the cop's personality, while at the same time heightening the overall "personality" or tone of the moment.

The **personality bite** is often fragmented, off the cuff, and informal. It is meant to infuse energy as much as, if not more than, it conveys story or character information. It keeps things alive and fun. It is there to remind the viewer that they have shown up to be entertained above all else, and that is what we aim to deliver—entertainment.

The Forecasting Bite (Color Commentary)

Storytelling and scene building must always take into account the bigger picture. If there is content within your raw footage that supports or indicates or "telegraphs" where your scene or your show's overall story is headed, generally you'll want to work it in (we discussed this in Chapter 1). A choice interview bite can reinforce this effort. And no bite is more effective at doing this than the **forecasting bite**.

A **forecasting bite** predicts how a relationship or a conflict within a scene might progress or grow in the scenes to come. In some ways this bite is very similar to the perspective bite, but it is so often used, and is such a convention of reality TV that it demands to be singled out and dealt with separately.

EXAMPLE:

```
          COP
This drunk seems harmless now, but something
tells me he's going to be a handful down at
the station.
```

or

```
          COP
Something seems off with this guy. I wonder
what I might find when we fingerprint him
down at the station...
```

Assuming there will indeed be more drama to come down at the station (drama that will pay off these bites), either one of them could help focus your scene and set up what will follow. A reality scene can be quick-moving and at times highly distracting for the viewer. A great

forecasting bite not only helps keep your story on track, it also keeps the viewer looking ahead and anticipating what is to come.

The Character Details/Background Bite (Play-by-Play)

When we first introduce a character in a show, it is common to employ a **character background bite** to relay pertinent pieces of information about his or her past. These details help to paint a fuller picture of the individual and flesh out that person's unique position and motivation within the show.

EXAMPLE: (NOTE—I'm going to step away from the cop/drunk scenario here to better illustrate)

```
                   JANE
     My name is Jane. I'm a single mom from
     Florida and I've been working as a junior
     chef for five years. My Dad is a chef and my
     grandfather was a chef, and I'm here to take
     it to the next level.

                   or

                   DICK
     My name is Dick. I am 32 years old and I have
     been struggling with an addiction to prescription
     drugs for 10 years. I've been in and out of
     rehab and I'm here to get clean for good.
```

When we, as the audience, emotionally invest in a character, we are not investing in his or her actions or appearance, we are investing in that individual's STORY. Where did she come from? What kind of life does she lead? Why is she here? Character background bites are essential for turning characters into individuals and personalizing their stakes.

Also, these bites can be invaluable when dealing with large ensemble shows that house MANY CHARACTERS. If you are watching a dating show full of beautiful young women, it is easy for them to blend into one another. But if you continually reinforce that Sally is from Texas and loves playing country music, and Denise is a single mom from Pennsylvania who has a hard time trusting men, and Lisa is a former Lakers cheerleader from Los Angeles who now owns a bakery, suddenly these characters are completely divergent and easily distinguished.

These bites are not limited to a character's background. Any objective DETAILS relayed about any character, at any time, fall within this category. Remember, as you consider employing such bites, it is always important to keep the overall story and CHARACTER ARCS in mind. Often there is an established direction in which things are going, a conclusion you are building toward, AND a journey that each major character is taking within the story. Character detail/background bites are key to establishing and developing these journeys. They allow you to check in, monitor, and report on the concrete changes that the characters are going through.

EXAMPLE:

> BIGGEST LOSER CONTESTANT
> When I came here I was 400 lbs. Now, can you believe it, I'm only 310. I've lost 90 lbs. in 3 weeks!

> or

> TYRA
> A week ago Tina was packing her bags and threatening to leave. Now she is out on that runway standing tall, strutting her stuff, and beaming with pride. She is fierce!

Character detail/background bites reinforced by strong moments of character-rich reality footage are essential building blocks of good storytelling. We want to identify with, care about, and/or disdain the people that we are watching, and we want those people to be fully fleshed-out, three-dimensional individuals. We want to be invested in WHOM we are watching just as much as WHAT we are watching.

The Reset Bite (Play-by-Play)

All reality shows are broken up into *acts*. Between each act is a commercial break. Often, when ending an act and going to a commercial, you will stop MID-SCENE, at a point of high tension and/or uncertainty: The bachelor has proposed to a lady, and she's just about to answer him. The contestant apprentices have gathered and Donald Trump is about to reveal which one is to be fired. (This mid-action pause harkens back to the way tension was built in the days of the old movie serials, the classic "cliff-hangers.") When we return to the show after the commercials we will often need to remind the audience of where we are and what has just transpired. After five minutes of distracting commercials, refrigerator runs, and bathroom breaks, we need to quickly recapture the viewers' attention and thrust them back into the action. This is when we employ a **reset bite**, which quickly and succinctly recaps the last few moments of story leading up to where we are now and reorients the viewer to reenter the action.

EXAMPLE:

Let's return to our Cop/drunk example to illustrate. Let's say that the cop is taking the drunk into custody. Then, all of a sudden, the drunken man lets it slip that he's an escaped convict on the lam! Now this is a pretty dramatic revelation and a great moment to "cliffhang."

It could play out something like this:

> Our cop lifts the drunken man to his feet. The drunk stumbles about and laughs uncontrollably. The cop begins walking him to the squad car. Suddenly, under his breath, the drunken man slurs...
>
> > DRUNK
> > **I can't go back. I just busted out.**
>
> Our cop freezes in his tracks and does a double take.
>
> > COP
> > **What did you just say?**
>
> ACT BREAK. CUT TO COMMERCIAL:
>
> RETURN FROM COMMERCIAL AND CUT TO:
>
> Our cop lifts the drunken man to his feet. The drunk stumbles about and laughs uncontrollably.
>
> CUT TO RESET BITE:
>
> > COP
> > **So I just stopped a suspect on the side of the road. He's been acting very strangely and clearly he's very drunk. I need to get the guy to my car and check him out.**
>
> CUT BACK TO SCENE:
>
> Suddenly, under his breath, the drunken man slurs.

>   DRUNK
>   **I can't go back. I just busted out.**
>
> Our cop freezes in his tracks and does a double take.
> He turns to the drunken man and attempts to clarify.
>
>   COP
>   **What did you just say?**
>
> AND WITH THIS, THE SCENE CONTINUES.

In this example events within our scene took a surprising turn. A secret was revealed. To keep the audience drooling for more, we cut away mid-scene, just after this REVELATION. We went to a commercial break. And when the show resumed we repeated the last few moments of action from before the break and used a **reset bite** to reorient the viewers and get them back into the action.

The Narrating Bite (Play-by-Play)

The **Narrating Bite**, which literally tells the story, beat-by-beat, action-by-action, is arguably the weakest use one can make of interview in a scene.

All play-by-play bites should be used sparingly, and this is especially the case with the narrating bite. People don't want to HEAR about the story secondhand. Show, don't tell. They want to SEE it play out. They want to experience the presumed reality of the moment. Sometimes, though, you have no choice. Sometimes to realize your scene's or your show's greater plan you must use a narrating bite because you simply don't have crucial story elements available to you in the raw footage. Without that crucial footage you can't cheat your scene, and you can't reshape or improvise in a new direction. You are left with a glaring hole, right in the middle of your plan. And in order for your scene to make complete sense you need a character to explain the exact details of the missing moments via a narrating bite.

EXAMPLE:

Let's suppose we are going through the raw of our cop/drunk scene and making our pulls. We have the cop arriving and finding the drunk. And we have the initial interrogation. But then the camera shuts off and doesn't turn back on for a full fifteen minutes! By this time the drunk is passed out in the back seat of the squad car, and the cop is wrapping things up with his dispatcher.

We don't have footage of the drunk getting up off the ground. We don't have him being taken to the squad car. WE DON'T HAVE HIM SAYING THAT HE JUST BUSTED OUT OF PRISON! We don't even have the cop calling into the dispatcher and asking about the guy. We only have the dispatcher's response.

In this example the scene would play as follows:

A cop approaches a drunken man on the street and says hello. The drunk takes one look at him and starts laughing. The cop looks him over suspiciously.

CUT TO NARRATING BITE:

                COP
      At this time I don't know what's going on
      with this guy. But he's drunk, so I stand
      him up and begin walking him over to the
      car. On the way, would you believe it? He's
      so drunk that he actually admits he just
      busted out of jail! I stop in my tracks and
      do a double take. Then, once I realize this
      guy might be for real, I cuff him, throw him
      in the back seat, call central, and ask if
      they have any jailbirds on the loose.

CUT TO:

Our cop is in his squad car, radio in hand, listening intently. Suddenly the dispatcher says...

            DISPATCHER (OS)
      Affirmative. We have multiple units dispatched
      and looking for him now. He escaped custody three
      days ago. Get him back here on the double!!!

With this, our cop steps on the gas and revs the engine.

As you can see in this example, by going to a **narrating bite** we've lost all of the interesting story actions and details that help make the scene memorable. There simply is no substitute for the real reality of the moment. But because such a crucial moment of story was missing, and because it was an essential piece of the greater puzzle, we were forced to use a bite that narrated what was going on in the scene, beat by beat, in order to maintain clarity, keep the scene moving, and get to the next crucial part of the narrative.

WAIT—WHY DID WE JUST COVER ALL OF THIS?

Why is it so important to understand the different categories and various narrative uses of the interview bite?

Once you rough out the content of your scene, you will step back and assess your narrative and feel out what is lacking—what it needs to be complete. Then you'll think about how to incorporate interview bites. By knowing the different types of bites and the ways in which each will uniquely affect your scene, you can confidently go looking for just what you need. Should we hear from Bethany or Sonja? Does the scene call for a little color commentary boost or the concrete clarity of a play-by-play bite?

In the same way, when searching for and selecting a bite, you often will be faced with more than one option. A few different characters might have been interviewed about the same event. Their commentaries might run the gamut from EMOTIONAL STATE to CHARACTER BACKGROUND, and it will be up to you to assess the scene, appreciate the different effects that each bite will have, and then make the strongest choice for your story.

Take Note: The Hybrid Bite

As you go about searching for that perfect interview bite to support your scene, you will often find that quite a few bites are hybrids (or combinations) of more than one type or category. You might have a bite that both expresses EMOTIONAL STATE and serves as a FORECASTING of what is ahead:

"Standing here watching this I am terrified; my housemates definitely seem unstable. I hope this isn't going to blow up in my face at some point."

You might have a bite that both RESETS a scene and simultaneously gives you CHARACTER DETAILS and BACKGROUND information.

"So I was in the midst of finishing my dish and Padma suddenly walked right in for a surprise challenge. Good thing I'm a single mom of a four-year-old. At least I'm used to the unexpected!"

Although individual bites may be hybrids, this should not change your approach to them. True, they may be affecting your narrative in multiple ways, but all that means is that you have to judge them on multiple levels. Don't be afraid of hybrid bites; sometimes they work even better than bites that serve a singular function.

QUICK, GET ME A BITE *STAT*!

As we know, not every plan works out exactly the way we'd like. Roadblocks and obstacles in the footage often require creative solutions. Many times we must cheat and rearrange to solve the problem. Sometimes we even need to deviate from the plan and move in an entirely new direction just to make the scene work. These are all important and necessary ways of getting the job done, but just as helpful, and sometimes even more valuable, can be the strategic insertion of a choice interview bite.

We've just illustrated how effective the interview bite can be at adding drama, texture, and clarity to a story. But it can be just as valuable for overcoming technical and structural problems within your plan.

Below is a list of technical uses for the interview bite:

PASSAGE OF TIME: Often the actual events of a story or scene will take place over a much longer period of time than the editor has to tell it. You might have to cover hours of material in mere minutes of screen time. In these cases an interview bite can be called upon to help compress the events. By inserting a choice bite you can step out of the action of the scene, distract the viewer, and then reenter at any point you wish and continue on from there. It's amazing how much a viewer will forgive if the right bite can distract them.

EXAMPLE:

Let's once again look at our cop scene. Let's imagine that, in reality, the cop ran the drunken man through a series of sobriety tests before cuffing him and taking him to the car. As we navigate the raw we discover these tests took FOREVER, are endlessly boring, and most significantly, are unimportant to the story we are telling. To keep the scene moving and the audience engaged, we need to bypass this tedium and jump ahead. The strategic insertion of an interview bite can help us do just that.

It might play like this:

```
A cop approaches a drunken man on the street and says
"Hello." The drunken man takes one look at him and
starts laughing.

CUT TO A BITE FROM OUR COP

                    COP
     I've seen drunks and I've seen DRUNKS! I ran this
     guy through a few sobriety tests and guess what?

CUT TO:

A CU of the cuffs being snapped onto the drunken man
and the cop leading him off to the squad car.
```

With a choice bite we were able to skip past all of this time-consuming content and move right to the next beat in our story.

Passage of time is a tricky business. Keeping the audience's attention, while expressing your story clearly and moving them from one point to the next, is a delicate craft. Too much time in one place or too much attention given to one story point can run the risk of dragging the whole scene down and boring the viewer. That's the last thing you want, because if you lose the viewer you lose everything, including potentially, your job!

CHANGE OF LOCATION: Not only can the raw footage for a single scene last hours that need to be condensed to minutes, it can also traverse many miles and various locations that also may need to be streamlined. Here again, a well-chosen interview bite can soften these transitions by either distracting or reorienting the viewer.

EXAMPLE:

Let's imagine that once our cop realizes his drunk is a jailbird, he radios in and discovers that a key witness is at the precinct RIGHT NOW waiting to finger this guy. The cop needs to get his drunk back to the precinct ASAP.

Okay, great, but the cop is nowhere near the precinct. So what do we do? Are we going to play out the action of our cop DRIVING all the way back to the precinct, pulling the drunk out of the car, bringing him up to booking, and having him processed into the system, all just to chronologically get to the next meaty bit of story? Of course not. Remember, time is of the essence in these scenes. There is no room for fat. Plus, the audience has no patience for those sorts of procedural minutiae. They want to see the drunk in that line-up already! So what do we do? Well, the easiest solution is, of course, a BITE.

It might play something like this:

```
Our cop drags the drunk back to his squad car, throws
him in the backseat, hops in the front, and goes for
the radio.

                    COP
          2019, this is 1854. I have an intoxicated male,
          white, 30 years of age, saying something about
          busting out of jail. Have you had any reports
          of an escape in the last few hours?

                    DISPATCHER (OS)
          1854 that's an affirmative. We have a female
          witness standing by for a lineup now. Need
          him back at the station ASAP.

                    COP
          Copy that, en route.

With this, our cop steps on the gas and revs the engine.

CUT TO A BITE FROM OUR COP:

                    COP
          When I hear the words witness and lineup,
          that means get back to the station and fast!

CUT TO:

We are now in the police station and our drunken guy is
being led into the lineup. The nervous witness stands
behind a two-way mirror, waiting to do her duty.
```

In this example we were able to skip an entire car ride with an interview bite. We were able to leap right to the next important beat in the story and bypass the business in between. By doing this we are able to keep the viewers' interest and not make them wade through unimportant details to get there.

CONTINUITY AND CHEATING: As I've said before, reality editing is all about the cheat: Mixing, matching, flipping, flopping, cutting out, and cutting down, all are a part of the game. Your job is to tell the most concise, dramatic, and focused story possible—in any way you can.

When the dust settles on this kind of approach there will no doubt be continuity problems aplenty. You might be mixing and matching moments that are shot hours apart and at different locations. And when you play your edited sequence back you may find that a character's position, demeanor, or even outfit may abruptly shift mid-scene. Obviously, in order for the scene to play you need to HIDE these sudden changes and jarring jump cuts. (The editing term "jump cut" refers to the joining of two film or video images that are ALMOST the same. Oddly, viewers find this more jarring than cutting between two completely different images.) For smaller continuity issues, a good reaction shot or some choice B-roll (an old film-industry term that designates any secondary or supplementary footage, such as non-essential shots of people or places or things) might do the job. For the bigger shifts, cutting out of a scene to an interview bite can be the perfect distraction for a little sleight of hand.

EXAMPLE:

Let's say that when our cop first approaches the drunken man, he is wearing his police hat and jacket. After a brief interrogation, the cop runs back to his squad car to retrieve a Breathalyzer. While he's at the car he REMOVES his jacket and hat before returning. As we've already decided to disregard all sobriety tests for pacing purposes, we now have a problem. One minute our cop is talking to the drunk and wearing a hat and jacket; the next minute he is not! You can bet the audience is going to notice this, and it's going to pull them out of the moment. BITE to the rescue!

It might play like this:

```
A cop, wearing a jacket and hat, approaches a drunken
man on the street and says "Hello." The drunken man
takes one look at him and suddenly starts laughing.
```

```
CUT TO A BITE FROM OUR COP:
                    COP
    I've seen drunk and I've seen DRUNK! This guy
    could barely stand, let alone answer a single
    question. Obviously he was going to need to
    sober up downtown.

CUT TO:

The cop, now jacketless and bareheaded, quickly
drags the suspect to the squad car and deposits him
forcefully in the backseat.
```

Again, by stepping out of the moment and cutting to a bite, we are able to avert the viewer's focus long enough to keep from jarring them with the shift in continuity.

There is one other thing to mention. A part of the trick with hiding continuity problems is exactly when and where we cut back into the scene. In our example we didn't return to the cop just standing in the same place, asking the same sorts of questions. Instead, we chose to cut back into the ACTION at an especially ENGAGING moment. The cop's on the move, his pace has accelerated, there's a heightened sense of urgency as he aggressively tosses the drunk into his squad car. Not only is the audience distracted by the bite, but once they reenter the scene they are forced to quickly reengage with a high-energy moment and CATCH UP WITH THE STORY. They don't have time to sit back, take it all in, and start picking out differences in continuity.

MISSED/MISSING PLOT POINTS: On the technical front, raw footage is often full of sound and picture problems, ready to undermine your plan at every turn. Perhaps the sound is too low and rough to clearly hear what someone is saying. And perhaps WHAT that someone is saying is essential to your plan. Perhaps there are too many things happening at once, confusing the viewer as to what they should be focused on. Perhaps the camera turned away from a key moment too soon, or couldn't reach it in time. This is when an interview bite can really save the day.

By inserting a well-chosen play-by-play bite you can quickly make up for any potential confusion and keep your viewer on track. In essence, you are reiterating and enhancing a story point for the purposes of ensuring narrative clarity.

EXAMPLE:

Our cop lifts the drunken man to his feet. The drunk
stumbles about and laughs uncontrollably. The cop begins
walking the drunk to his squad car. Suddenly, under his
breath, the drunken man slurs…

DRUNK

I can't go back. I just busted out.

BUT just as suddenly, simultaneously in fact, a
second police car arrives. Its lights flash and
siren BLARES!!! The siren drowns out everything else,
including the drunk's jaw-dropping admission!

AT THIS MOMENT WE CUT TO A BITE FROM OUR MAIN COP
SAYING:

COP

**Wait, did I hear this guy right? He just
busted out of jail?**

In this example, due to an audio obstruction, it is necessary to include an interview bite to drive home the obscured plot-point. Sure, we can subtitle what the drunk says, but this is a HUGE moment. The confession that he has just busted out of jail is key plot information. And because the arrival of the second police car, with flashing lights and a blaring siren, is such a distracting moment, there is just too much of a risk that the viewer might miss it.

RESUSCITATING A SCENE: This may not be entirely technical, but I still think it bears mentioning here. I can't tell you how many times I have constructed a strong and dramatic scene plan and jumped headfirst into the raw only to land smack-dab in the face of utter MONOTONY! Sometimes reality is boring. There's no kinder way to put it. Sometimes the characters are low energy, or the event is just not as gripping on screen as you imagined it to be on paper. Sometimes there are no cheats that can make it better, no restructuring that can give it life, and no deviations to save the day. Sometimes you are simply STUCK, and because your plan is a necessary piece of a greater puzzle, you have no choice but to embrace the banal and make a half-assed, underwhelming scene. Or do you?

As I explained above, choice interview bites (especially choice COLOR COMMENTARY bites) are a great way to heighten the drama of a scene and infuse some much-needed energy. This is never more of a necessity than in the face of narrative monotony. If a character seems uninspired in scene, find an inspired bite. If a moment lacks emotion, use an emotional bite. This won't solve all of your problems, but it will certainly go a long way toward keeping an otherwise DOA scene alive and afloat.

REDIRECTING THE SCENE: Imagine you are cutting a scene in which a contestant has just been eliminated from a competition. You have been given the directive that your scene must depict his anger and frustration at being cheated and betrayed. But there's a problem. As you begin to pull your selects you discover that THE GUY WASN'T UPSET! In truth, he was relieved and kind of giddy about the whole thing. That's an issue. It flies right in the face of your directive. And by directive I mean: **What your boss is expecting to see when he watches your cut!**

So what do you do???

Often, when the raw doesn't go the way you need it to, a few choice interview bites and some reality repurposing can turn things around. If the character expresses in a bite (even if it's out of context) that he's angry, you might be able to use this as a springboard to cheat the moment. If you can combine this bite with a few of his more serious expressions, you might be able to suggest the emotion you need. Trust me, even the giddiest of guys will have moments when his mouth is shut and his smile is down. Used out of context and married to the right bites, this may be all that's necessary to cheat the moment. The audience will feel the emotion of the bite and apply that to your strategically chosen images.

Obviously, this doesn't work every time, but you'd be surprised how often it does. Audiences want to believe what they're seeing. They want to embrace the fantasy and enjoy the ride. As such, they will often give you just the benefit of the doubt you need to get away with a little carefully conceived misdirection.

INTERVIEW RESOURCES

In order to USE a bite you first have to know how to FIND one. There are four basic resources that one can use to locate and isolate bites. Which of these you will have at your disposal really just depends on the job and the production company.

SCRIPT SYNC: This is the newest and, in my opinion, best way to search for interview bites. Quite often, a production company will employ a group of *loggers* whose job it is to *transcribe* every word of the interviews from the footage into a computer program.

The Script Sync program connects (syncs) those words with your interview footage via time code. All you need to do is open the transcribed document on your computer screen, double click the section you want, and the corresponding footage will pop up on your monitor. Pretty great!

Script Sync is especially helpful when you are cheating, or trying to replace specific words or phrases in an interview bite that may not have been delivered to your liking. Being able to word-search and then instantaneously hear how the possible alternatives were delivered saves a lot of time. (We will get into this further in the next chapter.)

TRANSCRIPTS: This is fairly similar to Script Sync, but without the whole *double-click and there it is* part. Transcripts are basically just the typed-out interview in document form. You can get it as a printed hard copy or as a Microsoft Word file. I prefer the file, in which you can conduct ever-important word searches. If you are searching for bites about Kate Gosselin's kids, for example, being able to quickly search every time she actually said the word "kids" can get you that much closer, that much faster.

STORY PRODUCERS: As I've said repeatedly, your greatest allies in the edit are the producers who have been assigned to collaborate with you. They are there to help guide and support the process, and one of their most valuable roles is that of "bite finding." That is a part of their job, and you shouldn't shy away from enlisting them to help you in this regard.

That said, I honestly prefer to do most of my bite searching myself. Just as with pulling selects, the more you explore the interview, the better you get to know it, and that can serve you exponentially down the line. Also, the more bites you are responsible for selecting and implementing on your own, the better you will be at doing it. I really only turn to the producer for bite help when time becomes an issue. If I have a hard deadline and my bite searches are costing me too much edit time, I will then ask my producer for help. Otherwise, I really do prefer to tackle it myself.

THE WATCH DOWN: Much like pulling selects, if all else fails, if there is no Script Sync, no transcripts, and no available producers, then you must dive into the raw interview on your own. You must watch through it all and pull interview selects, much as you would pull reality selects. Honestly, this is a last-case scenario, and a very TIME-CONSUMING one, especially if there are multiple characters and MANY hours of interviews. But if you have no choice, you have no choice. Them's the breaks!

NOTE: The only other time you may need to WATCH DOWN complete raw interviews is when you are dealing with a troublesome interviewee. I've dealt with subjects who are very poorly spoken and/or extremely low energy, which are both potential scene-killing traits. The last thing you want is an interview bite that no one can understand or that sucks the life out of a scene. In these cases I will watch down the character's entire raw interview and pull every last bit of usable bite from anywhere, about anything, and throw it all on a Timeline. This way, if I'm forced to use them, at least I know I'm using the very best stuff there is—IN or OUT OF CONTEXT.

Which brings me to my next point.

YES, EVEN BITES CAN BE TAKEN OUT OF CONTEXT

As is now becoming a mantra of this book: EDITING IS ALL ABOUT THE CHEAT. It's about taking elements out of their original context and giving them a new one, and this most definitely extends to the interview bite.

Normally, when assembling your scene you will have at hand portions of interviews that speak directly to the story you are trying to tell. Sometimes multiple people will be queried about the same event, and you will be able to pick and choose from among them. Even so, no matter how much interview material you have, chances are you'll still need more. Interview footage, just like raw reality footage, is never neat, clean, and simple. Quite often the bites you end up using in your edit will be, at least in part, completely out of context.

> ### In the Bay:
> Imagine we are cutting a romantic dinner scene between Hank and Kendra. In the midst of gazing into one another's eyes, we cut to a bite from Kendra saying, *"I'm so happy. I can't believe how lucky I am!"* To the audience watching at home she's referring to her marriage and loving husband. Only we know that this snippet of interview was actually stolen from another day and used completely out of context. She was actually discussing a big *Maxim* cover shoot she had just booked. It doesn't matter. If it works, it works. If the audience buys it and you have delivered the goods, you've done your job.

I am going to delve deeper into this kind of repurposing in the next chapter. For now, just know that in reality TV, the interview is as prime a candidate as anything else for a good cheat.

ONE MORE TIME: LESS IS MORE

However you opt to use interview footage, note that it is not only a powerful tool, it is also a precarious one. A little goes a long way. A few choice streamlined bites, used sparingly, will lift your work to new heights. Too many interview bites, used indulgently, will bury your work in lifeless tedium.

"Less is more" also applies to the length of each individual bite. No one bite should ever run longer than *absolutely necessary* to convey the information you *need* to convey. Trim the fat: Tighten every word, every "um" and "aw," as well as every breath and pause. Cut your bite down to its barest of bones. If it feels as if it's playing too long—it is! If you can't streamline it, find an alternative. If a bite feels redundant—it is! Have it make your point as succinctly as possible and move on. If your scene feels interview heavy—it is! Cut back on these bites or find different solutions to your problems.

Think of interview bites as if they were hot chili peppers that you are adding to an otherwise mild dish. A small amount can give your dish a zesty kick, but too much will render it inedible.

CHAPTER 5 REVIEW

Choose the correct answers from the lettered list.

1. In reality TV, what are the two essential categories of interview?

2. When returning from a commercial break, the editor will often employ a _____ bite to reorient the viewer to reenter to the action.

3. Perhaps the most powerful secret weapon that reality TV possesses is the _____ ____.

4. The interview can be effective at upping the drama, adding texture, and clarifying the story. But it can be just as valuable when overcoming _____ ___ _____ problems within your plan.

5. What are the four basic resources that one can use to locate and isolate good interview bites?

6. If you are dealing with an important story beat, the _____ __ ___ _____ is ALMOST ALWAYS much more engaging, emotive, and memorable than any interviewed recollection of the event.

   a. Interview bite
   b. Script sync, transcripts, story producers, the watch down
   c. Technical and structural
   d. Reality of the moment
   e. Reset
   f. Color commentary and play-by-play

Answers: 1-e, 2-d, 3-a, 4-b, 5-c

WATCH AND LEARN

Go grab a recorded episode of your favorite reality show, a piece of paper, and a pen. I want you to start from the beginning and watch through the show. As you go, try to identify at least five of the following NARRATIVE USES for the interview bite.

- The Perspective Bite
- The Emotional State Bite
- The Personality Bite
- The Forecasting Bite
- The Character Details/Background Bite
- The Reset Bite
- The Narrating Bite

CHAPTER 6

THE FRANKENBITE

I had considered including this next discussion in the previous chapter, but felt it was too important to be squeezed at the end of another, albeit related, topic. Yes, the term **FRANKENBITE** (also spelled Frankenbyte) does deal with the use and manipulation of the interview. But more than that, it serves as an example of how powerful non-linear editing can be, and how the reality TV editor truly is a television writer and storyteller.

WHAT IS A FRANKENBITE?

So what is a Frankenbite? Simply put, a Frankenbite is an interview bite that has been CONSTRUCTED from fragments of otherwise UNRELATED interview material. It is a sentence or series of sentences MANUFACTURED (i.e., tacked together) in the edit, as opposed to a sentence of series of sentences actually captured "in reality" on set.

As mentioned in the previous chapter, many bites are streamlined, tweaked, and augmented for the purposes of polish, but a Frankenbite goes far beyond that. A Frankenbite, much like Frankenstein, is made up of many different and often unrelated parts. It is a wholly new creation. And it is often the saving grace of an otherwise terminally challenged scene.

We've already discussed how, by isolating moments of picture and sound and breaking them down to their most basic elements, we can then use those elements to suggest new and different thoughts and actions. This is called CHEATING. A Frankenbite follows the same logic, but takes it to a more extreme level. In a Frankenbite, words—even word fragments—are elements to be drawn from and manipulated any which way needed to best tell the story.

In Chapter 4 we looked at an example from *Jersey Shore*. We split Snooki's line *"Hi there!"* into its separate words, *hi* and *there*. Then we took the word *there* and used it in a completely new context in a completely different moment and scene. Now, instead of Snooki saying, *"Hi there!"* we have a scene where JWOWW asks, *"Where's the bourbon?"* and Snooki responds, *"There!"* We have broken a whole into its parts and then used one of those parts in a completely new and different way.

With the Frankenbite, however, you not only isolate a word for use in another context, you PIECE TOGETHER a number of individual, out-of-context words to create entirely new statements! You quite literally put words in people's mouths.

In the Bay:

Let's say you are editing a scene from E!'s *Keeping Up with the Kardashians*. It's a scene between Kim and her sister Khloé in which Khloé is going on and on about her trying day while Kim sits silently nodding, her face expressionless. [Note: Our scene, like most of those presented in this book, is purely fictional and does not represent or refer to any actual scenes or interviews from *Keeping Up with the Kardashians*.]

In the midst of Khloé's rant you would like to cut to an interview bite from Kim saying, *"I hate Khloé. I really can't stand her!"* This bite is key to the scene because it gives the audience crucial insight into how Kim is REALLY FEELING. It reveals the true emotion beneath her expressionless nod. Your only problem is that SHE NEVER SAID IT! It's not there. You just don't have those lines. Or do you?

Here are three completely unrelated excerpts from an interview with Kim, and within them are all the elements necessary to create the bite you so desperately need:

BITE 1: *"**I** buy couture and **I** love it. Some people might **really hate** me for saying that, but it's true."*

BITE 2: *"**Khloé** is the youngest, but if you ask **her,** she'd say she's the most mature."*

BITE 3: *"And she looked at me like...**stand** up! You **can't** sit there all day!"*

As you can see from my highlighting, every word you need to create the statement is there. You just have to see each word as its own non-linear (out of temporal context) element, which can be manipulated any way you please to serve the needs of your story.

The illustration on the next page shows how this Frankenbite is constructed.

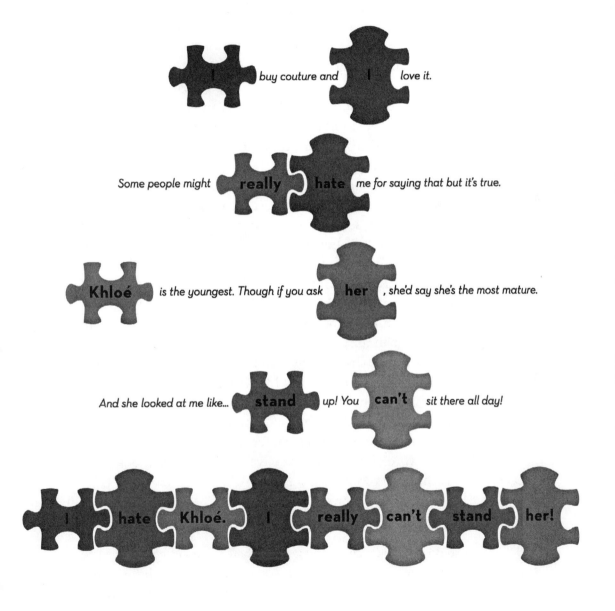

IF YOU DON'T BUY IT, THEY WON'T EITHER!

If used properly, the Frankenbite can be a game-changing device for an otherwise defective scene. But beware: Building a smooth and believable Frankenbite is no easy task. It is an art form, and one that you MUST master.

As we know, human beings stress words differently for a variety of reasons. One's mood, one's intention, even one's physical state (e.g., worn out, drunk, half asleep) can alter one's delivery in subtle yet most significant ways. It is essential to take this into account when constructing a Frankenbite. There is no greater "believability buster" than a poorly constructed Frankenbite.

If the audience catches on to a fake or fabricated bite, they will immediately stop focusing on the story and start focusing on the man behind the curtain—you! So close your eyes and listen to your Frankenbite objectively. Does it sound natural, or does it sound edited? Be honest, and above all, be critical. If you don't buy it, they won't either!

If you create the FRANKENBITE: *"I hate Khloé. I really can't stand her."*
But instead it plays: *"I HATE Khloé. I REALLY can't stand HER."*

The emphasis is on the wrong words, and it feels like a constructed statement—not like natural speech.

The good news is that, chances are, within your interview footage there are quite a few versions of the word "I," perhaps a dozen of the word "really," and possibly even a handful of the word "hate." Therefore, it is crucial to TRY EACH WORD, option after option, until you find exactly what you need to make your Frankenbite feel real and sound right. (Note: Transcripts and word searches are very, very helpful when looking for each use of each needed word.)

THE BEST-LAID BITES...REWRITTEN

What do you do if you just can't find a good "hate" or an effective "really"? Do you bag the bite? No. Do you see if you can get away with the bumpy Frankenbite you already have? NEVER! Remember, reality TV editors are writers, so if you can't find the exact phrase you need—rewrite it. There are many different ways to express a sentiment. Try them all until you find one you CAN turn into a perfectly believable Frankenbite.

If you need *"I hate Khloé. I really can't stand her"* but you can't make it work, try instead *"I don't like Khloé. She really annoys me"* or *"Khloé is such a bitch! She drives me crazy"* or *"Khloé sucks. She makes me want to explode!"* You are expressing the same sentiment, just using different words.

So how do you find these different words? You do it by scanning your transcripts and searching the raw interview. You search for choice words and turns of phrase that speak to the spirit of your bite. Reality TV editing is all about staying fluid and flexible. You must always remain open to what comes. Real life is unpredictable, and you need to stay limber enough to bob and weave with the tides.

USE YOUR MORAL JUDGMENT

I have one last thing I'd like to discuss about Frankenbiting. (Quite honestly, it also applies to ALL aspects of cheating—although it's especially pertinent here.) Frankenbiting can be a highly effective device, but it can also be a harmful one. You are changing the words coming out of people's mouths. You are making them say things that they never said and perhaps never would say. And as your work is for a television show that will ultimately be seen by millions of people, you must always ask yourself and your superiors: IS THIS CHEATING CORRECT?

Solving problems, breaking through obstacles, and seeing your work come to life can no doubt be invigorating. But don't be seduced by them. Be sure you are not crossing any moral lines as you manufacture dialogue for reality characters. Now, don't get me wrong, this isn't a common problem. If you are working WITHIN THE SPIRIT of the character, fabricating dialogue specifics should not be a problem. If you do them right, your cheats and Frankenbites will heighten and REINFORCE your show's reality, not completely CHANGE it. But be prepared to face moments when you must look to your better judgment and back away from a solution that could do more harm than good.

CHAPTER 6 REVIEW

Choose the correct answers from the lettered list.

1. There is no greater _____ than a poorly constructed Frankenbite.

2. An interview bite that has been CONSTRUCTED from fragments of otherwise UNRELATED interviews is called a _____.

3. A reality TV show is generally viewed by millions of viewers. As such, when constructing a Frankenbite, you must ask yourself "_____ _____?"

4. Remember, reality TV editors are writers, so if you can't find the exact phrase you need, _____ __.

    a. Frankenbite
    b. "Believability buster"
    c. Rewrite it
    d. Is this correct?

Answers: 1-c, 2-a, 3-d, 4-c

CHAPTER 7

MUSIC

"Music in reality TV isn't something that should be playing in the background as if someone left the radio on in the kitchen. The music should KNOW what scene it's in, listening and changing with the turns in the story."
Sax Eno, Editor,
Hell's Kitchen and *The Real World*

I remember quite clearly the first time I really began to appreciate music editing. I think I have always had a respect for music in my cuts. And I have certainly strived to choose pieces that would generally support or fit my scenes. But it took a few years before I was exposed to REAL MUSIC EDITING.

I was working on a show called *Fashion House* for a division of Fox Television. It was a short-lived experiment with prime-time soap operas. Basically, Fox had purchased the rights to a bunch of Spanish-language *telenovelas* and was adapting them into English with 1980s-era stars like Bo Derek and Morgan Fairchild. It was a pretty intense experiment in that, just like working on a regular old soap opera, we were charged with creating an hour of television EVERY night! As such, there was a lot of work for a lot of editors.

One of those editors was a guy named Sax Eno, who had come from the world of Fox reality TV, having been a lead editor on shows like *Trading Spouses* and *My Big Fat Obnoxious Fiancé*. At the time, I was still working my way up and he was a rung above, working as a "finishing" editor. This basically means that he would take my cuts and the cuts of others, and finish or POLISH them up for air. The great benefit of this type of relationship is that I would get a chance to see how a more experienced editor adjusted and improved upon my work. Remember, you never stop learning as an editor, and perhaps the biggest lesson I learned from Sax was in the art of MUSIC EDITING.

I quickly came to realize that Sax was a master with music. Where I might choose a cue that seemed BASICALLY to fit and slap it under some picture, Sax was much more calculating. For him, music was a whole other—and equally important—CHARACTER in the story. When he placed music within a scene, he did so specifically and deliberately. He wouldn't just select a music cue and drop it in place. Instead, he would assess each section of a chosen cue, and then break it apart, stretch it out, cut it down, and even combine it with other cues. Each musical moment was positioned just so—in order to perfectly support each and every moment of the story.

Sax taught me, by example, that music is just as malleable as picture, dialogue, and interview—and just as powerful. As you cut in music, you are quite literally SCORING your drama. I know that sounds obvious, but reread it. You are SCORING your drama. Really take it to heart. Think about what it really means. When editing music, always choose it carefully, position it deliberately, and never be afraid to break it down, mix it up, and experiment.

RESPECT THE CUE

Great music editing will ELEVATE your work and your demand in the marketplace. The right music choice can turn light drama into devastating heartbreak and simple humor into gut-busting hilarity. It can accentuate your pacing and reinforce your rhythm. It can produce vibrant moods and powerful emotions where they might otherwise be severely lacking. Music is not just an ingredient, it is a whole separate organism that, when paired effectively with your picture and dialogue, can give your scene or whole show true LIFE.

Used incorrectly, however, music will not only lose its power, it can actually undermine everything you have worked so hard to accomplish with your show's other elements. The wrong music cue can turn heart-wrenching drama into zany comedy and edge-of-your-seat tension into yawn-inducing boredom. Music is a primal form of artistic expression. It is hardwired into our bodies and hearts. If the wrong music is used in a scene, that moment is forever emotionally translated incorrectly.

KEEPING THE RHYTHM (A.K.A. TAPPING IT OUT)

Here's a little exercise for you. Take a piece of music, something basic, like a Beatles tune. As it plays, start tapping your foot to the beat. Pay attention to the song's change-ups and when they occur. When does a lyric begin? When does it resolve? When does the chorus kick in? When do the instrumentals take over?

You'll notice that there is a very discernible pattern that repeats itself in most basic musical cues. By tapping your foot you will be able to predict exactly when that chorus will kick back in and how long that instrumental section will last. This is an important exercise to practice because music editing is all about making your edit AT THE RIGHT SPOT.

When you cut a music cue down or expand it you will change its structure, but you should never change its basic beat—what you tap your foot to. When listening to music, most people are tapping an invisible foot in their heads. They'll spot a bad cut a mile away. A jump cut in the picture can be jarring and off-putting, but not nearly as jarring as an offbeat, out-of-rhythm cut in the music, which can be musical suicide. So, as you choose your cutting points in a cue, tap your foot. Cut on the beat. And when you review your work let your gut, your internal metronome, be the judge. Have you preserved the cue's rhythm? Have you kept its flow? Can your foot keep tapping through your music edit?

A well-used music cue can actually mask questionable edits in picture and dialogue, but NOTHING can mask a poor edit in the music itself. Remember, when viewers experience a bump in the musical road, it will jar them to their core. They might SEE a poor picture edit or HEAR a poor dialogue edit, but they will FEEL a poor music edit.

THE SEVEN DON'TS OF REALITY TV MUSIC EDITING

When discussing music and music editing in a book of this scope, I think it's best to cover the short list of important DON'Ts rather than the myriad DOs. To be honest, I could write another whole book on the DOs. But for now, while covering all the basics, I'll hit on the major mistakes and pitfalls that must be avoided.

Reality television music editing has seven primary don'ts:

1. SKIMPING THE CUE
2. THE LAZY LOOP
3. THE CARELESS "CUTDOWN"
4. "TONE" DEAF
5. MISSING THE TURN
6. THE POOR MAN'S TRANSITION
7. WALL-TO-WALL

1. Skimping the Cue

The first thing any editor must do before working with a piece of music is LISTEN TO IT! Now this sounds obvious, right? Unfortunately, it is the most common mistake that a less experienced editor will make. Too often the editor will play the first few moments, decide it's good enough or not good at all, and push forward. This kind of rash decision-making is what I call **Skimping the Cue**, and it does you and your story a HUGE disservice.

Music is full of MOVEMENT and CHANGE. Each piece of music develops, repeats, and resolves in its own way. And often a shift or change can be quite unexpected. Sometimes this can be a good thing: That high-energy cue might kick into even higher energy—driving your scene to a thrilling climax. And sometimes this can be a NOT-SO-GOOD thing: That high-energy cue might abruptly switch into a soft melodic ballad—grinding your scene to an immediate and unintentional halt. For this reason it is imperative that, just as the editor must WATCH ALL OF THE RAW before cutting it, he or she must also LISTEN TO THE WHOLE CUE before making a decision about it.

Just because a cue starts off wrong doesn't mean there isn't a golden section just a few measures away. Conversely, just because a cue opens well, that doesn't mean that some off-putting, distracting, and totally inappropriate change-up isn't looming right around the corner. Listen to the complete cue, know what you're dealing with, and then make an informed decision. Put in all the time that you can spare to do it right.

Once you become more experienced you will be able to scan through a track a bit more quickly, perhaps at double speed. You will start to recognize the repeats, when the chorus comes, and how the cue's changes occur. You will begin to streamline the process.

2. The Lazy Loop

Next to uncooperative musical shifts within a cue, the most challenging aspect of music editing is duration. A cue is almost NEVER the exact length you need it to be. Sometimes it's too long and you have to cut it down. And sometimes it is too short and you need to LOOP it.

Looping is the duplication and repetition of a cue or portion of a cue. It is done when you need to "stretch" the music to fill an amount of time that's longer than the cue or the portion of the cue you choose to use.

Looping is essential when you are editing shows that are driven by commercial pop songs. During my time at MTV I was constantly running into this. The production had licensed, and thus wanted to use, as much popular and recognizable music as possible. The big problem was that pop songs are FULL of lyrics. And when you are scoring a scene full of important dialogue and interviews, a loud Taylor Swift screaming, "WE ARE NEVER EVER GETTING BACK TOGETHER," can be a tad distracting.

In this type of situation you have to scan the track—whole track—isolate the lyric-free instrumental portions, and then loop it to fit your scene. As lyrics can cover up to 90% of a commercial pop song, chances are that the instrumentals you pull will be fairly short—so looping will be your only option.

Looping is an important and necessary tool for extending the usable portion of a cue to cover your scene, and it can quite often be a cue saver. But there is a danger in looping: Once you have a strong piece of looped music that works well for your scene, it heightens the scene's drama and accentuates its emotions, so there is a tendency to want to squeeze that loop for all it's worth, to stretch it out for as long as possible. But this is a risky thing to do because a loop is a just a short repeating section of music, and as with any other type of repetition, too much is TOO MUCH. It can become a cue KILLER! Just as the right amount of well-chosen and fluidly edited looping can really serve a scene, too much of it can make it feel monotonous, and even irritating. The editor who commits the crime of over-looping is guilty of the **Lazy Loop**—trying to squeeze too much juice out of a single loop in order to avoid the work of finding more cues.

Nothing frustrates me more than polishing the work of another editor who has covered his or her scene with lazy loops. Sometimes I'll receive a six-minute scene with ONE PIECE OF LOOPED MUSIC! An average cue is only a minute and half. Looping just a small section of that cue for six minutes? Come on! I guarantee that's not an editor that I will ever recommend.

3. The Careless "Cutdown"

As mentioned, the length of your cue will often differ from the length of that which you are trying to score. Sometimes the music will be too short and require a **loop**. Other times it will be too long and must be cut down to fit. It is this act of CUTTING A CUE DOWN that I want to discuss here.

Remember, most cues are full of shifts and changes. Sometimes these changes can abruptly move into unusable territory, sabotaging your scene. Halfway through your somber death scene an otherwise appropriately somber music cue could suddenly kick into a high-energy upbeat rock, and that's the last thing you want! But just as often, the music's shifts and changes will be subtler—they'll be variations on the same mood that will add texture and diversity and dynamism to your scene. In these cases, when you cut down a cue that WORKS well with the scene, carefully assess it and make use of as many of its WORKING PARTS as possible.

The problem is that many editors don't take the time to do this. Quite often, if they find a cue that WORKS, they will simply drop the thing in, let it play until they need it to stop, and then just fade it out. This is the **Careless "Cutdown"** and it does your scene a terrible disservice.

In the Bay:

When I streamline or cut down a cue that works well with my scene, I will once again listen to the whole thing. I will not just slap the thing into place and let it play out. I will assess each verse and each chorus. Then I start my streamlining, trying to make use of the music in ways that best serve my scene. I may trim a little here and balance that out by trimming a little there. As I cut the cue down I do my best to preserve the music's shifts and changes that give my scene dimension.

Think of it like getting a haircut. Barbers and hairdressers don't simply cut along the base of your hairline and say, "Okay, it's shorter." They make numerous little adjustments. They balance one section with the next. In a sense, they condense your hair, not just snip off the bottom and call it done.

Of course, reality TV music editing is not an exact science. At a certain point, you may still have to cut to the chase and slap that ending on there, or fade the thing down, but the more of the cue's integrity you can preserve, the more dynamic it, and your scene, will be.

4. Tone Deaf

Another important music editing DON'T: Don't be **Tone Deaf**. Now this is not the traditional use of the term "tone deaf," but it is certainly related. The tone I am speaking of is the *emotional tone* of the drama you are attempting to score. Is it a happy moment? Is it a tense moment? Is it comedic? Is it tragic? Identifying and matching the dramatic tone of the sequence with the proper music to score it is essential.

To clash the tone of the scene with the tone of the music beneath it is a potentially scene-killing crime. You would never put sad music under a comedic scene, uplifting music under a death scene, or scary music under a wedding (unless you wanted the music to clue the audience to some odd subtext of the scene). It's like having a guy faint, and then cutting to a shot of a woman yawning. It doesn't connect. The viewer would be puzzled and might disconnect from your story.

Reality TV can get a bit more complex than just "funny" and "scary." A reality scene can portray an infinite number of emotional DEGREES. Therefore, when selecting the music to underscore your scene, you must listen carefully in order to find just the right pieces to match the emotions you are trying to express.

> ### In the Bay:
> Let's look at an example and try to apply this idea of DEGREES of emotions within a scene. Let's say we are scoring a scene from Bravo's *The Millionaire Matchmaker*.
>
> For the moment when the Millionaire has just started his first date and there seems to be a spark between him and the woman he's paired with, you might use a HOPEFUL cue.
>
> For the moment at the end of the date when the Millionaire gets cappuccino foam on his nose but doesn't realize it, you might use a TICKLED cue.
>
> And for the moment when the Millionaire has his first real kiss of the date, you might choose an ELATED cue.

> All of these cues may be considered emotionally "positive," yet each one clearly represents a different DEGREE or shade of positive. It is important to understand and learn to make these subtle, subjective distinctions. You must be as emotionally specific as possible when selecting a cue.

Often the only way to really nail the perfect cue is by trial and error. You may actually have to cut multiple options against the scene to SEE and FEEL which ones work best. In reality TV editing, however, time management is always an issue, so you can't spend all day searching for the perfect cue, especially if you already have some options that generally work. But spending as much time as you can spare, and getting the closest cue you can find to the dramatic tone of the sequence, will make a big difference.

5. Missing the Turn

The next DON'T in music editing is a crucial one: **Missing the Turn**—letting a music cue drift on past its emotional appropriateness. In other words, the scene takes a left turn, but the music continues on a straight path.

As we all know, a scene is not made up of just ONE emotion. A scene is a journey that often covers a spectrum of emotions.

> ### In the Bay:
> Let's say we're cutting a scene from TLC's *Here Comes Honey Boo Boo*. As the scene opens we see Sugar Bear (Honey's dad) arrive home, EXHAUSTED AND GLUM after a grueling day at work. He drags himself into the house with a sigh. Then, all of a sudden, he freezes. He notices that his usually boisterous home is eerily dark and totally silent. He calls out. No answer. He calls again. Nothing! His demeanor turns DEAD SERIOUS. He begins moving from room to room, speeding up his pace as his heart begins to race.
>
> Then, suddenly, as he enters the living room... "SURPRISE!" The lights pop on and his entire family jumps out. He sees piles of presents beneath a "Happy Birthday!" banner. His state of worry vanishes and is replaced by the biggest SMILE OF JOY you can imagine.
>
> This is all one scene, but within it there are three very distinct emotional TURNS. To highlight these turns the experienced editor will score each with its own tonally appropriate music cue.

As Sugar Bear enters the scene we might use something sluggish, even monotonous, to reinforce his downtrodden state. When he discovers that his home is eerily abandoned and begins moving from room to room, we might turn to something tense, dramatic, and suspenseful. When he discovers his birthday party, we might transition to something happy and celebratory. By paralleling each of Sugar Bear's emotional TURNS musically, the audience will truly FEEL as he feels, and this is crucial to the success of the scene.

Imagine if you were to keep the slow, monotonous music going once Sugar Bear has discovered his home abandoned, or worse, keep it going even after he's discovered his surprise party! To miss these TURNS would be to confuse your drama and completely undermine your scene.

Imagine a sad, defeated cue playing, not just when a player thinks he's lost *The Amazing Race*, but continuing to play even after he discovers he's won! Imagine a comedic cue playing, not just when Paris Hilton is chasing her soapy dog around the bathroom, but also throughout the unexpected phone call she suddenly receives from her angry father. Picture a dramatic cue playing, not just when Tyra Banks reveals a daunting *America's Next Top Model* challenge, but also after she says, "Just kidding! Today you guys actually get a spa day to relax!"

Before scoring any scene, identify all of its dramatic shifts, beats, and TURNS. This will help you avoid letting a cue OVERSTAY ITS WELCOME! The more precisely and subtly you score the scene the more dynamic it will become, and the better your story's emotional impact will translate to the audience.

6. The Poor Man's Transition

Most scenes contain various emotional turns. To accentuate these turns, it is often effective to reinforce them with similar turns in the music. The point at which you change from one cue to another is called a musical TRANSITION point. I've stressed the importance of knowing WHEN to make your musical transitions, but it is equally important to determine HOW to make them.

When I first started editing I discovered a handy trick. When I identified a dramatic TURN in emotional tone and needed to change a music cue, I would simply fade the first cue out and abruptly cut to the next. Then I would lay a loud cymbal swell (a crescendoing roll on a cymbal, which in this context could be called a sound effect) over the cut to mask it. This trick can be quite effective, and the cymbal swell has become a convention of sorts in reality television. Unfortunately, it is one of the most overused and abused "short cut" devices in the genre. It screams "WE ARE TRANSITIONING!" Picture an entire scene or, worse yet, an entire show in which every music transition was "hidden" by a cymbal swell. Might get a little irritating, right?

This all-too-easy, hackneyed transition is just one example of what I call the **Poor Man's Transition**. When you take the easy way out of a cue, you rob yourself of the option to do something far stronger, more dramatic, and more musical. There are any number of ways to transition from one cue to another. Some require careful and deliberate music editing; others might exist organically within the cue and simply require you to just open your ears to take advantage of them.

Digging out an interesting and unusual *musical sting* is a perfect example of the latter. (A *sting* is any short, isolated musical phrase, or even just a single note or chord that is usually used for dramatic effect.) Many cues end with great *natural* stings, e.g., one final smash of the drums or twang of the guitar that slowly "rings out" to silence. These can be great elements to play with for creating more natural, less over-used transitions, AND for accentuating dramatic beats within a scene. When Donald Trump says, *"You're fired!"* and we edit this to coincide with a final dramatic boom in the music, the audience feels the emotion of this moment tenfold.

Another great transition is the *musical dropout*. It's a classic reality TV convention that is especially useful in comedic situations. The musical dropout is a sudden, unexpected end of a cue. For example, music is simply playing along, accompanying the picture, when out of the blue, something ridiculous happens on screen, and the music suddenly stops (i.e., DROPS OUT). It has basically the same effect as suddenly cutting to the sound of a phonograph record skip/screech (as if the needle had been suddenly swept off the record) or suddenly cutting from boisterous music to the placid, nocturnal sounds of crickets. As long you choose your edit point correctly (remember to tap it out, cut on the beat, keep the rhythm), this can be a great way to punctuate a moment and really dial up the humor.

There are many different ways to manipulate your cue to create powerful moments of transition, and most of them will honestly just take some experimentation. You hear something, you have an idea for a transition, and you try it out. This is how it works, and this is how you grow. BUT you will never grow if you don't give yourself the chance. By just fading something out willy-nilly or worse, cutting abruptly from one cue to another without forethought or care, you do not serve the emotions of your scene. Remember, this is called MUSIC editing. It's about LISTENING to everything you have and manipulating it to realize its greatest potential.

7. Wall-to-Wall

A film or video that is scored more or less continuously, with few if any breaks from the music, is traditionally said to be scored **Wall-to-Wall**. This sort of unending use of music doesn't allow for actions and dialogue to play out on their own, which can sometimes be incredibly compelling without musical accompaniment. Instead, it bathes everything is a certain sameness.

The problem with this kind of approach to music is that can end up downplaying your scene's or show's drama. Just as with cymbal swells and overly repetitive loops, the more you use something the less dramatic its impact becomes. In other words: Less is more. Less score is often more dramatic than the wall-to-wall score. The entrance of music after a period with NO MUSIC can be a powerful thing. It says, "MUSIC IS HERE FOR A REASON, NOT JUST BECAUSE EVERYTHING HAS TO HAVE MUSIC." This can be a potent device, especially when you are trying to heighten a dramatic shift and give it as much resonance as possible.

Also, the absence of music can sometimes be a much more effective way to play a scene. If two people are racing through a tornado trying to reach their storm shelter, the wind, rain, hail, and general chaos of the moment might be lost by including an overbearing cue. (Note: To create the strongest scene, you must take care that music and sound effects—wind, rain, gunshots, etc.—do not fight against one another for the audience's attention. When they fight one another, they both usually lose.) If two people are having a romantic dinner by the sea, the crackle of the fire and the sounds of the surf might be all you want to retain the "sap-free" intimacy of the moment.

There is no exact science for when and how to place your cues and when to go "dry" (music-free). It really comes down to how you assess the drama of the scene you are scoring. What are the emotional hills and valleys of your story? When do you think music is necessary? When might it actually be overkill and too intrusive? And when do you think that delaying the music and introducing it later might serve to drive home a particular twist or turn in the drama?

WARNING: As with so many aspects of reality TV editing, or any creative pursuit, style and subjectivity play a huge role. Certainly, YOUR style and YOUR instincts are crucial. What may be even more significant, however, are the stylistic tastes of your boss and his or her boss—the Network. To this point, it is my experience that there are some producers and network executives out there who are uncomfortable with "music-less" reality. They need WALL-TO-WALL music to feel comfortable. They may not have enough faith in their audience or the material to trust that emotions and drama can be clearly expressed without a heavy and literal score. In these cases you must go against your better judgment and deliver what they demand.

Quick Tip: String Your Cues

As I've mentioned, searching for the right cue is time consuming. It is often a true test of editorial patience. Sometimes you must listen through fifty cues or more just to find the one that works. Here's a tip to speed things up:

Music cues are almost always separated out and categorized for the editor. There will be a series of computer bins, and each bin will house cues specific to a particular genre or tone.

The genre-specific and mood-specific cue bins available to you might look like the ones on the following page.

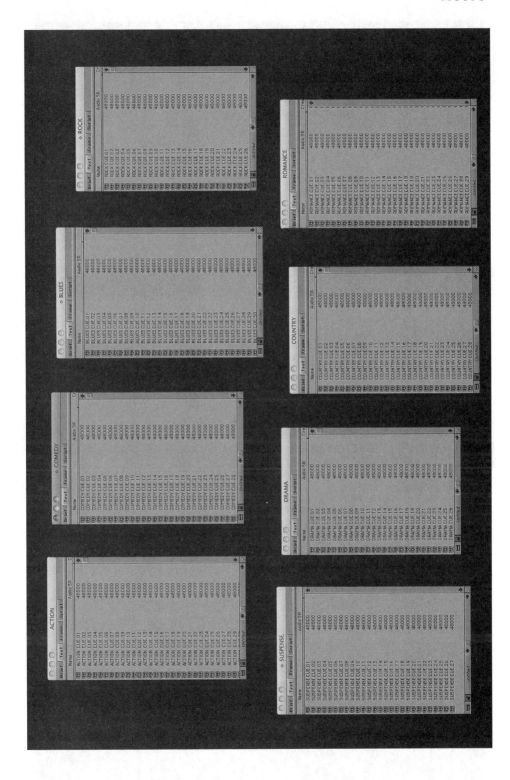

One helpful way to quickly listen through multiple cues is by opening a
bin and cutting all of its cues onto a single timeline.

**Here's an example of a music cue bin and its cues placed on
a timeline.**

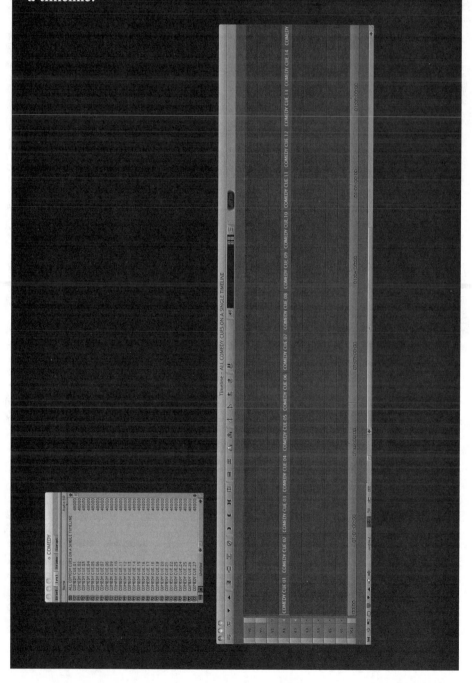

Once the cues are strung out back to back on a single timeline, you can easily skip from one to the next with a simple move of your mouse. Working this way, you are, in effect, scrolling through your music choices as opposed to opening each cue, one at a time, individually. Trust me, you'll be surprised how useful this method can be.

FINAL WORDS ON MUSIC

Music editing is one of the most overlooked and underappreciated tools in reality TV. It is also one of the most potent. It's amazing how many problems you can solve—and scenes you can save—with a firm musical grasp. The more you explore, the more you experiment, and the more you learn from the successes and failures of others, the more on track you will be to rising above the rest and becoming one of the best.

CHAPTER 7 REVIEW

Choose the correct answers from the lettered list.

1. When you cut something down or build something out, you are going to be changing the structure of a cue. But you should never change its nature or its _____.

2. _____ is when you duplicate and repeat a cue, or usable section of a cue, as many times as needed, to fit your scene.

3. To score something _____ means there are never any moments that go WITHOUT music.

4. What do you call the point at which you change from one cue to another?

5. Too often the editor will play only the first few moments of a music cue, then quickly decide it's good enough or not good at all, and push forward. This kind of rash decision-making is what I like to call _____ ___ ___, and it does you and your story a HUGE disservice.

6. Imagine a sad, defeated cue playing, not just when a player thinks he's lost *The Amazing Race*, but continuing to play even after he realizes he's won! This is an example of _____ ___ ___.

7. To clash the ____ of the scene with the ____ of the music beneath it is a potentially scene-killing crime.

8. Quite often, if an editor finds a cue that WORKS, he will simply drop the thing in, let it play until he needs it to stop, and then just fade it out. This is called ___ _____ _____, and it is doing your scene a terrible disservice.

a. The careless cutdown
b. Looping
c. Rhythm
d. Skimping the cue
e. Missing the turn
f. Wall-to-wall
g. The transition point
h. Tone, tone

Answers: 1-c, 2-b, 3-f, 4-g, 5-d, 6-e, 7-h, 8-a

WATCH AND LEARN

Go grab a recorded episode of your favorite reality show, a piece of paper, and a pen. I want you to start from the beginning and watch through the show. As you go, pretend that you are a famous and well-respected reality TV music critic who has been asked to review this show's use of music. It is your charge to critique the merit of each and every cue within it. Does the music work for or against the scene? Does it heighten the drama and build emotion or does it detract and distract? See how many of our seven "don'ts" you can find. I've re-listed them below for your reference.

1. Skimping the cue
2. The lazy loop
3. The careless "cutdown"
4. Tone deaf
5. Missing the turn
6. The poor man's transition
7. Wall-to-wall

CHAPTER 8

A LITTLE MORE AUDIO

Clearly, music is essential to the craft of reality TV editing. Not only can it elevate your story, it can often make or break a scene. But music is just the beginning of your audio landscape; there are other elements that, though not as evident, are just as important to the process.

SOUND EFFECTS

Sound effects (SFX) are among the most underappreciated, yet invaluable, elements in reality TV editing. They're underappreciated because they are not technically essential to your basic edit. A cut of a show can theoretically get by without them. But there's a big difference between theory and practice. And though SFX may not be essential to simply telling a story, they are absolutely necessary to telling a story in the BEST way possible. Strong "sound design" (meaning any and all SFX) can accentuate drama and heighten reality. Convincing SFX can add dimension, reinforce emotion, and magnify what is most captivating.

Choose Wisely

In the previous chapter I emphasized the importance of listening to as many music cues as possible before making a selection. This same rule applies to SFX.

On most editing jobs, you will be provided with a SFX library. This is a vast pool of sounds that have been sorted by subject into a series of "bins" (computer editing program's term for a folder). Within each of these bins you will often have various versions of the same type of sound to choose from. It is up to you to choose just the right sound for just the right moment.

You may have available to you five different "dog barks," ten different "gunshots," and fifteen different "brake screeches," but there may be only one (or even none) of these that blends seamlessly into the reality of your scene. You must have the patience to look at ALL of your options before making the best selection. The differences between them may be subtle, and you may have to try quite a few against picture to really see what works, but I promise you, in the end it will be worth the effort. An inaccurate, unconvincing, inappropriate, or otherwise out-of-place sound can be distracting, and can even pull an audience out of a moment. At the same time, a well-chosen sound—one that hits your ear and your gut just right—might be the key to nailing and truly selling that moment.

Foley and Background SFX

There are two categories of sound effect. The first and most prevalent are the **Foley and Background** sound effects. These SFX mimic and re-create the "soundscape" of the environment—the aural ambience and incidental sounds that naturally occur—where your scene takes place. Traffic noise, crashing waves, a door slam, a dog bark, footsteps in gravel, etc.: These are all Foley and background SFX that represent or stand in for actual sounds that occurred on your reality TV location.

Foley and background SFX add texture, detail, believability, and dimension to a scene. They can draw an audience in and convince them that what they are seeing is REAL. It's amazing how adding the PSHH PSHH PSHH of that sprinkler or the RAP-TAP-TAP of that man's typing fingers can impact a scene. These elements will also give you more material to manipulate for dramatic effect: If the traffic noise suddenly disappears, or the rain suddenly stops, you can be sure the viewer will take notice.

In the Bay:

Let's imagine you are cutting a scene for Fox's *Hell's Kitchen*. In the scene, a competing chef struggles to finish a dish while an impatient Gordon Ramsey watches in the wings. By adding in and then slowly increasing the sound of the BOILING BUBBLES as a chef overcooks his dish, or by inserting and then slowly raising the TICK TICK TICKING of a looming wall clock, a once dramatic scene suddenly becomes nail-biting!

You are editing a scene for Discovery Channel's *Deadliest Catch*. In it a crew of fisherman wrestle with an uncooperative crab trap as it's pulled from the icy waters. To heighten the intensity of the moment, you insert the sounds of ROARING WIND and CRASHING WAVES. By bringing these SFX to the foreground and making them so loud that they even drown out the frantic voices of the crew, a serious scene suddenly becomes a life-and-death battle against nature's fury.

By manipulating the level and intensity of choice **Foley and Background** SFX, you can affect drama and focus the narrative of a scene. That said, it is important to note that more often than not, subtlety is the name of the game with this type of sound effect. Nine times out of ten you want these sounds to be ABSORBED into the soundscape of the scene. There is a reason they are called "BACKGROUND": They are meant to help create and bolster a sense of reality, not stand apart from it.

Take Note: Respect Your "Nat"

Now that we've covered **Foley and Background** SFX, I want to discuss one of the most common sound-related mistakes in all of reality TV editing. When editing a scene it is crucial to establish and maintain the natural or "nat" ambience within it. These are the natural sounds of the environment where the scene is taking place. If a guy is walking through the woods, we need to hear the sounds of the woods (chirp-chirp, rustle-rustle, etc.) in the background. If a woman is walking down a city street, we need to hear the city sounds that envelop her. The consistent presence of these ambient sounds is essential to selling the reality of the moment, so they must REMAIN present and consistent from shot to shot throughout the entirety of the scene. That said, I cannot tell you how often I will receive an editor's work to polish, only to find shot after shot with absolutely no "nat" sound whatsoever. In fact, often these shots will have no sound, period! Nothing, just muted silence.

How does this happen? How could a shot end up in a cut with no sound? Well, as we've discussed, reality TV editing is all about the cheat. It's about cutting out of context. And out-of-context shots will often come married to very distracting out-of-context sounds. A typical out-of-context shot might have pieces of random, unrelated dialogue, the voices of completely foreign characters, and even distracting production crew chatter beneath it. Because of this, it is often necessary to strip the picture of its sound before cutting it into your scene. BUT, just because the native sounds have been removed from these shots doesn't mean that they don't still NEED sound if they are to be convincing. In order to blend various shots into your scene seamlessly, they must be given a consistent background ambience. If a guy is sitting in a noisy bar and you cut away to a close-up of his drink, you still need to hear the sounds of that noisy bar. It would be pretty weird not to.

So, when building a scene, always remember to RESPECT YOUR "NAT." Be sure that beneath every shot in your scene one you maintain the consistent and continuous background ambience of the moment.

Design SFX

The second category of sound effect is called the **Design** sound effect. This category is technically quite similar to musical score. These are sounds added to your edit that are separate from the reality of the scene. They are not meant to sync with or parallel any specific action; they are entirely foreign and play as a separate character intended to accentuate the drama. The loud BOOM of a bass drum, the cacophonous CRASH of a cymbal, or the eerie SHAKE of a rattle are all sounds that may have no literal relationship to your scene (which might be a boardroom in *The Apprentice*) but can still go a long way toward selling the emotion and drama of the moment.

As opposed to Foley and background, **Design** SFX are *meant to be heard*. They *can* be loud. They are *supposed* to stand apart. And reality TV is one of the few genres where they are prevalent and encouraged. You can have fun with these foreign, often larger-than-life sounds on a level that scripted television and movies could never get away with. Use of design SFX has become part of the reality vernacular, where it is an invaluable tool, heightening the impact of a moment and reinforcing the twists and turns of a story.

In the Bay:

You are cutting a scene for CBS' *Big Brother* and a contestant reveals, in interview, that she is secretly allying herself with her sworn enemy. A well-placed *BOOOOOMMM!* can do quite a bit to reinforce the impact of this revelation.

You are crafting some comedy for MTV's *Jersey Shore*. A drunken Snooki stumbles about, trying to appear sober for a Seaside Heights police officer. A well-timed cartoonish *BOING!* when she finally collapses, butt-first on the pavement, can make the punch line of the scene truly pop.

The use of design SFX can focus drama, punctuate comedy, and heighten emotion, BUT if you're not discriminating, that *use* can very quickly turn to *overuse*! Too many BOOMS, CRASHES, and SWELLS can quickly go from dramatically stirring to distractingly irritating. So use them wisely, sparingly, and appropriately. I've said it before and I will say it again: A little pepper can spice up a scene, but too much can render it inedible.

Quick Tip: Keep Your "Faves" On Deck

Every aspect of the editorial process must be weighed against one very important factor—the deadline. A great edit means absolutely nothing if you can't get it done and delivered on time. As such, TIME MANAGEMENT is essential.

To help with this I find it useful to have certain tools and elements as readily available as possible while I cut. Creating a bin on your computer and filling it with choice SFX is one great way to do this. Chances are there will be certain sound effects, perhaps a specific BOWED CYMBAL SWELL, that you will find yourself returning to again and again throughout the process. Sometimes they will be SFX that *you* feel are most effective. Other times they will be your *boss's* favorite SFX, or what other editors have already defined as the *show's* signature SFX. By gathering these sounds together and storing them in one easily accessible bin, you can save yourself loads of time when you need it most.

Reality editing isn't a casual stroll through the postproduction park; it's a race to the finish, and you need every bit of help you can get along the way. So, just as Batman needs his utility belt and Robin Hood needs his quiver of arrows, having an SFX "GO TO" bin can be invaluable when faced with mounds of work and very tight deadlines.

"VO" (VOICE-OVER)

The next audio element that I want to discuss is **Voice-Over (VO)**, which is an offscreen narration (i.e., the disembodied voice of someone not seen on screen) that usually describes or comments on something shown on screen. You'll commonly find it used in science-, geography-, and history-based programming, but it can pop up anywhere. In reality TV, VO is used in lieu of, and even sometimes in ADDITION to, the interview. And more often than not it serves the same purpose as the play-by-play interview bite discussed earlier in this book. It is a story-tracking tool, which is written and recorded in postproduction and left to you, the editor, to incorporate.

The great freedom and power that comes with VO is your ability to say whatever you please, however you please, and whenever you please. It is an entirely malleable device that is only confined by the limits of your imagination. Also, a VO-driven show can give you great flexibility with your footage, as you can *tailor* the words to not only fit your story, but also to support the particulars of and solve any problems with your raw. You can fill in story holes, bridge logic gaps, and reinforce subtle moments that might otherwise be lost.

As Always, Too Much Is...Too Much

Too much voice-over is generally not a good thing. Nothing is as effective as reality's raw footage. *Show, don't tell* is still the rule of the road. You should always make an effort to use the VO to *support*, not replace, the reality of the moment.

VO is used in quite a few danger-laden reality shows to ramp up the stakes. On Discovery's *Deadliest Catch*, for example, a stern and serious voice establishes the incoming weather and the looming dangers. It sets the scene's tone and moves the viewer from ship to ship as the show's various stories play out, but it does not take the place of the scene's reality. Instead, the VO sets the stage, while the reality footage brings the drama and characters to life, illustrating their personal struggles and real-time reactions, capturing the audience's attention and emotions and holding them through the episode's end.

There are, of course, exceptions to this idea of VO taking a backseat to the reality footage, but those exceptions are generally for shows that AREN'T *truly* reality TV. For example, if you are cutting an *E! True Hollywood Story* you would allow VO to play a large role. But this type of program is more a news magazine than a down-and-dirty reality show. It is journalistic TV, as opposed to REALITY. Will you be faced with this type of work? Perhaps. And if you are, understand that it is a slightly different animal, and not specifically what this book is about.

Respect the Scratch Track

VO is frequently developed in stages. As your cut evolves and changes, so too will the lines of voice-over that support it. And while the final version of your VO will often be recorded in a professional studio and performed by paid talent, its preliminary versions will likely be captured a little closer to home. And by "home" I mean in your edit bay. Likewise, the performer called upon to read early VO drafts will also be a bit more immediate, meaning you or your buddy down the hall. This rough "place holding" form of VO is called a **SCRATCH TRACK**.

It is important, however, not to take the term "scratch" too literally. The TECHNICAL quality of these recordings may be less than finished, but that doesn't mean the DRAMATIC quality should be. VO is a powerful element, and should be treated and READ with care. The moment that VO is inserted into your cut, everything changes. A new principal character has been added to the world of your story. A VO-driven scene can fly or flop depending on the strength of its performance and conviction of its reader. So get it strong and get it right every time. (This is a simple rule that will do wonders to elevate your work.)

A Few VO Pointers

Cast the Scratch: As stressed above, a strong VO read is important at every stage of the editing process. For this reason, be discerning and CAST YOUR SCRATCH. This means surveying the office and selecting someone with a strong, tonally appropriate voice and the dramatic chops to do your script justice.

Know the Equipment: Every editing room is outfitted with a mixing board and an omnidirectional microphone for recording VO. But from bay to bay you will find differences in the way things have been set up. The button or switch that activates the mic in one bay may be completely different from the dial or fader that activates it in another. For this reason, whenever you start a job, familiarize yourself with this equipment. You never know when you'll have to fire up that microphone and record a quick line at a moment's notice. The last thing you want to be is a fumbling editor, confounded as to why things aren't working—especially when your boss is in the room.

Watch the Levels: Before your vocal talent starts a read, test his or her volume levels. You have a meter and a mixing board at your disposal, so make the most of them. I always have my narrator read his first few lines as a test at the volume and intensity he intends to read the whole text, and then adjust my mic levels accordingly. Recording something too low is annoying, but usually salvageable. Recording something too hot is jarring, and often renders the material distorted and unusable. Take a minute and make some simple adjustments before you begin. You'll be glad you did.

Heed the Pops: When recording VO, watch out for audio POPS. These are the unsettling *PUHS, BUHS*, and *THUHS* that can often accompany words beginning in those perilous consonants. When recorded, especially by a closely placed mic, they basically sound like distorted little explosions of air. The microphones that we are provided are generally not the best. They don't have windscreens or shields to soften the sound and lessen the pops. What you get is what you get, so once you've recorded your VO, play it back, and make sure you got it POP free. If not, record it again, but this time have the performer angle away from the mic slightly when they come to the POP-producing words in the script. Usually this is all that's necessary to fix the problem.

Mark the Script: It's great when you can find a scratch narrator with some acting experience, but this is generally a LOT to ask of the average dude across the hall. As such, it will be up to you to guide their read, directing them on what to stress and how to stress it. One helpful tool in this process is what I call "marking the script." This simply means scanning the page for each and every word that needs to be stressed, and underlining it for your performer. Singling out the key stressed words will go a long way toward helping your newfound thespian navigate the page successfully.

Stand Them Up: One of the key elements to any good VO read is energy. A lackluster read is like a limp handshake: uncomfortable, distracting, and detracting. If you find that your narrator is a little too sleepy for your liking, one quick solution is to STAND HIM UP. Take the mic off the stand and get him on his feet. You'll be amazed by how much more alive a reader will become with this simple adjustment.

Embrace the "Line Reading": To give a performer a "line reading" is to say the line aloud yourself and then tell that individual to simply mimic your inflection and intonation. You are, quite literally, showing the performer how to say it by reading it yourself first. This is a serious no-no in the world of acting, but in the world of SCRATCH VO, the line reading can be a lifesaver. I guarantee you will run across lines that your narrator just can't figure out. In those cases, save yourself some hassle and just give it to him. Trust me, it's much better than having a misread line of VO in your cut.

Use the Best Takes: I know this might sound like a no-brainer, but too often editors will record a bunch of VOs, doing take after take of each line to get it right, and then drop the ball when cutting it in. They'll play it back, and then go with the first read they come across that sounds halfway decent. They won't take the time to listen through everything and select the very best takes (and sometimes fragments of takes) possible. Once again, just as with music cues and SFX, be thorough. Have patience. Listen to each and every take you have, and choose the best pieces to give your scene the strongest VO possible.

THE MIX

"If your producer can't hear it, it didn't happen."

Anthony Rivard, Editor,
Top Chef and *The X Factor*

The **Mix** is the combination of all of a scene's or show's constituent audio tracks—production sound, dialogue and interview and voice-overs, ambience, SFX, music, etc.—at appropriate relative volumes. In a good mix, all of the aforementioned audio elements are balanced correctly to make the scene understandable and moving. Dialogue must work with and float above the music score. SFX must be present, but not TOO present— unless their purpose is to startle the audience. From moment to moment and from shot to shot, the mix must always serve your audience's overall viewing experience of the scene and/or episode.

Too often the inexperienced editor will disregard the mix of his scene with the belief that, since everything will be remixed and sweetened (a term which includes adding reverb and timbre refinements) at a sound house (a mixing facility), there's really no point. This is completely WRONG. The best way to shoot yourself in the foot, and destroy everything you've worked so hard to build, is by distracting your boss with a terrible mix. *"What is he saying? Is there music here? OWW! My ears are bleeding! This scene needs a lot of work!"*

What we hear and how we hear it has a tremendous effect on the way we experience a scene. If the music is too loud, it can drown out your story. If it's too soft, it can sound like a mistake. Low dialogue can be irritating and distracting, while dialogue that peaks with distortion is often too jarring to absorb. Therefore, you must carefully watch through your whole scene and adjust each and every audio element in each and every section. Great editorial choices can be lost to a lazy mix. Conversely, a STRONG MIX can pull your work together. It can intensify drama, focus story, and capture the viewer from beginning to end.

Blasting the Scene

One common rookie mistake that I see again and again in mixes is the tendency to BLAST THE SCENE. An inexperienced editor will go through and properly balance each sound in relation to the others, but then will crank the overall volume to 11! They often do this because they are insecure about the quality of their work, and are hoping that the sheer power of the volume will mask the lack of actual drama within the scene. Or, worse yet, mask their inability to deliver that drama.

Some producers can be momentarily fooled into thinking a LOUD scene is a POWERFUL scene. I mean, our ears, and by extension our bodies, DO have a natural reaction to LOUD NOISE, but this effect won't last for long. So, it's better to keep things at non-deafening levels from the start, recognize the weaknesses in the scene, and address them. That's how you learn. That's how you get better.

Burying the Music

Another common mix-related misstep is BURYING THE MUSIC— playing music too quietly in the mix. This seems to occur when a less-than-confident editor worries that the music selection is off, and instead of taking the time or seeking the guidance to get it right, he or she simply lowers the music's level to such an extent that the listener can barely tell it's there, let alone what its tone or intention might be.

Unlike BLASTING THE SCENE, this is a mistake that your boss, and any other viewer, WILL notice right away. There are few things more distracting or aggravating than knowing there is music and not being able to make it out. It's as if someone has added mysterious flavoring to your favorite dish. You know it's there, but it's so subtle you just can't place it. You want to enjoy your food but you just can't. The mystery is too distracting.

FINAL WORDS ON SOUND

A strong soundscape is one of the most underrated yet significant dimensions of any great edit. It is amazing how much can be suggested, focused, and expressed through choice SFX, commanding VO, and a strong MIX. I always say that a great scene should play just as powerfully with your eyes closed as it does with your eyes open. This is a medium of image AND sound. Embrace that and use it to your advantage. Attending to your sound with the same level of care as you do your picture will only serve to improve your editing, your standing in the workplace, and your career as a whole.

CHAPTER 8 REVIEW

Choose the correct answers from the lettered list.

1. The loud BOOM of a bass drum, the cacophonous CRASH of a cymbal, or the eerie SHAKE of a rattle are all sounds that have no literal relationship to your scene. As such they are considered what kind of SFX?

2. What term refers to the way in which all of the various sound elements and their respective volumes are working together within the finished cut?

3. A rough "place holder" or temp VO is called a _____ _____.

4. Attending to your _____ with the same level of care as you do your picture will only serve to improve your editing, your standing in the workplace, and your career as a whole.

5. What kinds of SFX are intended to mimic the literal environment that you are attempting to create?

6. What is used in lieu of, and even sometimes in ADDITION to, the interview, and more often than not serves the same purpose as a PLAY-BY-PLAY interview bite?

7. When less experienced editors worry that their music selections are off, they sometimes lower the music's level to such an extent that the listener can barely tell it's there. This is called _____ ___ _____.

a. The mix
b. VO
c. Burying the music
d. Design SFX
e. Sound
f. Background and Foley SFX
g. Scratch track

Answers: 1-f, 2-a, 3-g, 4-e, 5-f, 6-b, 7-c

WATCH AND LEARN

Go grab a recorded episode of your favorite reality show, a piece of paper, and a pen. I want you to start from the beginning and watch through the show. Take note of any and all SFX you hear. Then write down what category each SFX fits into. Is it a background and Foley SFX or a design SFX? Try to find at least ten of each before you're done.

CHAPTER 9

WHAT CAN'T BE TAUGHT

(OR, HOW I LEARNED TO TRUST MY GUT!)

We have now covered all of the basics that go into reality TV editing. We've discussed the fundamental steps necessary to take raw footage and turn it into a strong, focused story. And we've covered the most important tools at your disposal for infusing that story with as much life, energy, and clarity as possible.

Okay, great, so now what?

Well, editing is a complex thing. So far we've discussed many rules and tips and tools and skills. But that's only half of the craft. The all-important other half of it involves your gut reactions, your intuitions, your sixth sense. These things cannot be taught from a book, but they can be sharpened and focused by experience.

Although we don't usually realize it, we've actually been studying the art of the edit all of our lives. Every movie, TV show, commercial, and music video has, in effect, programmed us with an innate sensibility and sensitivity for film and video pacing and flow. Growing up in an environment teeming with edited moving pictures has instilled in us all the potential to become great editors. And it is this ingrained sixth sense that is probably the most important and valuable tool any editor can draw upon, because, at its core, great editing is all about instincts.

You'll just *know* when you have been on one shot too long and need to cut to another. You'll *feel* when something plays too long or zips by too quickly. But make no mistake, just because we are wired with these instincts doesn't mean they don't require constant exercise. Just like most other skills discussed in this book, the more you do it the better you will be. In this case, the more you draw upon these instincts, the more attuned they will be and the more sensitive you will become to the choices and changes that constitute GREAT EDITING.

Okay, so now that I've established that instinctual editing can't be taught—let me "teach" you some stuff about it!

Below are a few of the more important "subconscious" elements to pay attention to as you build your scene.

PACING

As with a piece of music, visual storytelling is a living, breathing, emotional animal. An audience gives itself over to your "ride," and you must take full responsibility for their experience. A well-edited show should be a fluid experience. It should bring the viewer from beginning to end without calling attention to itself or undermining the story. It should carry its viewers effortlessly and leave them thirsty for more. This is why the rhythm and **PACING** of an edit are quite simply EVERYTHING.

Once you strike a *pace* (the general rate at which you present material: fast, slow, frantic, etc.), respect it, commit to it, make it consistent. If you choose to alter your pacing, make sure that change is motivated by what's on the screen. Only a dramatic or emotional shift in your story should justify such a change, and when you do make a pacing shift, do so fluidly. Think of it like driving with a passenger in your car. If you start out cruising along at 30 mph and then suddenly, for absolutely no reason, hit the gas—pedal to the metal—and then just as suddenly slam on the brakes, I can guarantee that your passenger will be jumping out at the first chance he or she gets. If you accelerate or decelerate, do so gradually, and with proper motivation, not just on a whim.

As an editor, you are the driver; your passenger is your audience. They expect you to give them a good ride, so choose your pacing carefully, stick to it, and make sure you have strong motivation for your changes to it as you build your cut. Then, after you're done, watch it back. Become the audience and see for yourself if it FLOWS. Did you enjoy the ride? Make it feel right for your gut and it will feel right for everyone else's.

In the Bay:

We are cutting a scene from *The Osbournes*. Jack Osbourne sits alone in his messy room eating cold day-old pizza. He is clearly bored. To reinforce his state, we decide that every shot should be draaaaaaawnnn out. Even the clock on the wall should seem to be ticking in slow motion. Commit to this choice. Feel the monotony. Embrace it.

Suddenly the phone rings. Jack sits up, waking from his daydream. As this constitutes a dramatic and emotional story shift, the cutting starts to pick up. Jack has snapped back to reality so the pacing now has more of a real-time feel. On the phone is the woman Jack's been trying to land forever, and guess what? She's coming over right now! Major beat shift. He jumps up and looks about. His place is a pigsty and he has to tidy up quickly. To reinforce his frenzy, our cutting pace picks up dramatically. Edits start coming at a pace equal to that of Jack's rapidly beating heart. Each shot is carefully selected, representing only the loudest and most colorful moments of his action. This fast cutting remains steady and consistent right up until DING-DONG! She's here! Everything comes to a halt. We linger on one shot—an extreme close-up of his flushed and nervous face. We stay on it for as long as it takes.

In this scene the rhythm of the cutting and the changes in its pace are deliberate and specific; they are not motivated by technical needs. They are in direct response to emotional and dramatic turns in the narrative. Each section of the scene has a committed and dedicated flow to its cuts. When the story demands a pace change, only then do the cuts comply.

POLISH

Reality television allows for much more flexibility than other genres when it comes to DIRTY CUTTING—which is the inclusion of wild pans and zooms, jarring cuts, etc., that call attention to the camera work and editing. In scripted TV the edits generally need to be invisible. You are trying to suggest an edit-less experience. Rarely, unless stylistically imposed, will you find shaky pans and snapping zooms in scripted television. You are supposed to lose yourself in the fantasy and have no sense of the "man behind the curtain." In reality television, on the other hand, a little bit of dirt is accepted—and even encouraged. It is, after all, an actual DOCUMENTED experience, and you can acknowledge this with a bit of dirty cutting. There WERE cameras and there WAS a crew. As such, a kinetic and raw visual style can actually heighten this *vérité* (realistic, naturalistic) feel.

This raw visual leeway can be of real benefit to a reality TV editor. Since raw footage is anything but cooperative or predictable, this license to jump, this freedom to jar, this permission to be a little less than continuous, is often just the flexibility a reality editor needs to make an otherwise troublesome edit work. That said, there is a huge difference between VÉRITÉ cutting and SLOPPY editing. Raw, rough, vérité editing is a craft, and one that should be practiced and mastered. The right snap zoom (*extremely* fast zoom in or out), focus jitter, camera whip (*extremely* fast camera pan), or stylish jump cut can escalate the energy and emotion of a scene. But, as is always the rule, less is more, and in this case, too much is MUCH TOO MUCH. Because of this, when assembling a scene of reality television, the editor should always try to make things flow as SMOOTHLY as possible.

Dirty cutting should always be an exception to the rule, not THE rule. Too many jarring jumps and bumps get old in a hurry. If you become too indulgent with your dirty cutting or too lazy to find a smoother way of presenting your material, your scene will go from feeling real and raw to appearing cheap and sloppy in a heartbeat. Try to make the smooth shots work. Try to maintain the scene's continuity. Try to avoid unnecessary camera jerks and focus pulls. Do what you can to maintain a polished and smooth overall style, but let your gut be the judge. Keep in mind that content is king, so you should never dismiss an amazing moment just because it cuts a little rough.

The rough and loose nature of reality TV editing is a tricky thing. Finding that perfect balance of clean and dirty, edgy and smooth is not something that can be taught. In the end it will come down to how the scene plays for YOU. It's all about your gut. You must trust yourself and your instincts to help you find the way.

Quick Tip: Edit on the Move

One very helpful tip to remember, especially when you are trying to soften some "rough" spots in your scene, is to EDIT ON THE MOVE.

If you are cutting from one shot to another and you fear the lack of continuity between the two might jar the audience, look for a quick pan, a camera jerk, a snap zoom, or even a movement from the subject in the frame. And, if you can, look for this sort of motion on both sides of the cut. You will be surprised how often this will make two seemingly discontinuous shots smoothly cut. I'm not sure why it works, but the eye just seems to forgive an awkward cut when it is mixed with a move. It is the ultimate iron for an otherwise glaring visual wrinkle.

EMOTIONAL CONTINUITY

As mentioned above, when you work through your edit you should TRY to make things flow as smoothly as possible. A part of this means attending, as best you can, to the visual continuity of a scene. If a giddy Shannon Tweed is holding a glass of champagne when you cut away from her to a smiling Gene Simmons, mid-toast, you do your best to have her STILL HOLDING THAT GLASS when you return. That's VISUAL CONTINUITY.

But there is another form of continuity that also must be adhered to, and that is **EMOTIONAL CONTINUITY**. If keeping the champagne in Shannon's hand maintains VISUAL continuity, then keeping the giddy spring in Shannon's step preserves her emotional continuity. To put it simply, emotional continuity maintains the consistency of a character's emotional state from shot to shot. This is an especially important concept to keep in mind when you cheat out-of-context reactions and actions. A cheated shot, by nature, does not originate from the same moment in time that the shot you are cutting from does, but both shots had better share the same emotional content.

Emotional continuity is a key factor in portraying a character's emotional shift within a scene. Much like my earlier driving analogy, a character must be allowed to shift naturally and organically from one emotional state to another. You can't cut away from a happy Shannon and then right back to a sad Shannon. You need to SHOW her move from one emotional state to the next in a real and believable way. The audience needs to SEE her transition to believe it, so always be sure your EMOTIONAL FLOW is as organic as everything else in your edit should be.

CUTTING THE STORY

As a young actor I spent many hours dissecting scripts in preparation for performances. And the most important lesson I learned was that, first and foremost, story is king. Every choice that I might make as a performer needs to be in the service of the greater narrative. Every look, every word, every action only exists to help support the journey of the whole. As such, I learned to ask myself two important questions at every step of my performance preparation: What is the ultimate story to be told? And, How can my interpretation of the script tell that story most effectively? This lesson has benefited me immensely as a reality TV editor.

As an editor, your primary responsibility is **CUTTING THE STORY**. From shot to shot and scene to scene your choices must always be driven by the larger narrative you are attempting to translate. When do you cut to a character speaking his or her mind? When do you cut to the reaction of another character listening? When do you cut away to an object of attention or a character's point of view? When do you stay wide? When do you move in close? Every cut you make has meaning—it SAYS something to the viewer. And it is your job to make sure it is saying the RIGHT SOMETHING.

In the Bay:

Sometimes CUTTING THE STORY is fairly clear-cut. Ozzy Osbourne yells at Sharon. We then cut to a close-up of Sharon for her reaction. Pretty straightforward, right?

But what if Ozzy yells a dozen things at Sharon? He complains that their house is a mess, that there's no gas in his car, and that his tee-shirt shrank in the wash. But it is only when he goes on to tell Sharon that she has no right to take a job and pursue a career of her own that she truly seems hurt. It is on this criticism that her eyes widen and well. This is the real meaning of the scene. This is the path that the drama is taking. This is the subtext. Ozzy doesn't care about the car or his shirt. He's angry because she took a job. She's chosen to make her life about something more than him, and this affects him deeply.

In this case, we might wait before we cut to Sharon's close-up reaction. We might hold off on using such a powerful shot until Ozzy gets to his REAL point. Perhaps we stick to mediums and wides as Ozzy rants about. And then, when he finally reveals himself—BAM! We cut to an extreme close-up of Sharon for her reaction. In this way we reserve the POWER of Sharon's close-up until just the right moment to help reinforce the true meaning of the argument. Thus, we use our images deliberately to help tell the story of the scene.

Editing is not meant to simply COVER events (i.e., give you just the basic facts); it is meant to SHAPE and FOCUS the story. You are a visual STORYTELLER. So you must know the big picture. You must know the purpose of each scene within this bigger picture, and use your instincts to show this with each and every cut you make. Then, when you have finished your edit, watch it through with the sound turned off and just focus on the picture. Ask yourself: "Am I visually translating the story effectively?" Only then will you have given your work the justice it deserves.

WE ARE ALL EDITORS

In *Outliers*, his *New York Times* best seller about successful people, Malcolm Gladwell asserts that for someone to truly master a skill he or she must dedicate 10,000 hours, or roughly ten years, to its pursuit. By this reasoning, I suggest that the vast majority of the American population has what it takes to judge the strength and merit of an edit before they hit puberty!

Growing up in the age of Netflix, YouTube, Hulu, cable TV, and the like has conditioned us all with the instincts of an editor. The most important aspects of visual storytelling do not come from formal rules, tools, or tips. They come from someplace much more basic—that most experienced editorial eye—our gut. As you work through a scene, always remember to FEEL it out. Trust your instincts, because you aren't just an editor; you are also an audience member. If you can make the scene feel right for yourself, you will make it right for everyone else.

CHAPTER 9 REVIEW

Choose the correct answers from the lettered list.

1. When assembling a reality TV scene, the editor should always try to make things flow as _____ as possible.

2. The very large part of the editor's craft that cannot be taught in a book is relying on your_____.

3. Once you strike a ____, respect it: Commit to it. Feel it out from shot to shot. Keep it consistent.

4. _____ _____ maintains the consistency of a character's emotional state from shot to shot.

5. Reality television allows for much more flexibility than other genres when it comes to _____ _____.

6. What is one very helpful tip to remember, especially when you are trying to soften some "dirty" cuts?

7. Editing is not meant to simply COVER events; it is meant to _____ ___ _____ story.

    a. Smoothly
    b. Pace
    c. Dirty cutting
    d. Emotional continuity
    e. SHAPE and FOCUS
    f. Edit on the move
    g. Gut

Answers: 1-a, 2-g, 3-b, 4-d, 5-c, 6-f, 7-e

CHAPTER 10

I GOT IT ALREADY!

The title of this chapter is not meant to reflect your current mindset. (If it does, I may be a better teacher than I thought!) This chapter is about the art of streamlining and tightening your story and your edit.

Have you ever noticed how many parents tend see their children through the distortion of "rose-colored glasses?" We've all heard it before: "Oh, there's no baby cuter than mine!" "Oh, my child can do no wrong!" Well, it's funny: The same thing can happen to an editor when looking at a supposedly finished cut: "It's perfect. There's nothing I could possibly lose. Everything is there for a reason." We fall in love with our work, especially when it is actually WORKING!

Crafting order, rhythm, and life from a seemingly random sea of raw footage can be a frustrating process. When you finally find shots that actually work well together and you start to see moments come to life and play as REAL TV, you naturally start to develop some strong emotional attachments to your cut. A strong working cut is a hard feat to manage, and when you get there, the last thing you want to do is tear it apart. But that's exactly what you must do. In reality TV postproduction (and in honor of deluded parents everywhere) we call it "KILLING YOUR BABIES." A little crude, I know, but I think you get the point, right?

> *"It's important to be emotionally invested in the scenes that you cut, but you also have to avoid being too precious. Quite often I will find myself blindly attached to my work even when the process suggests I remove it for the greater good of the story. It's a tough balance, but when in doubt, cut it out."*
>
> Sax Eno, Editor,
> *Hell's Kitchen* and *The Real World*

Once you have a cut that you feel confident about—with your picture and dialogue, your bites, your cheats, your music, and SFX all working together to serve your plan—it's time to take a step back and ask yourself: What do I *really* need to tell this story? What is *essential,* and what is tangential? What is reinforcement, and what is repetition? What is golden reality drama, and what is merely treading water? And most importantly, how much time do I have to play all this out? Often you will be given time constraints that will force you to make "hard cuts," and these constraints are usually NOT suggestions. It is not only your job to deliver the best cut possible, it is also your job to deliver that cut "TO TIME."

"Once I finish cut. Once I've watched it down and feel confident about each and every shot. That is when I have to ask myself the most important question of all: Is it to time?"

Anthony Rivard, Editor,
Top Chef and *The X Factor*

REVIEW YOUR PLAN

Returning to your original scene plan can be invaluable to this process of streamlining and tightening. That plan and its outline will help remind you of the core story you set out to tell. By looking at your outline's key points and comparing them to your "finished" scene, you will more clearly identify the moments that are essential and those that are excess.

Let's look at an example of using the plan to trim a scene's fat. Return to our club scene from earlier in the book and imagine we've just completed our first cut, and it seems to be working really well.

Here's how the finished scene plays:

A guy walks into a club. He looks about the room and spots a beautiful woman sitting alone at the bar. He removes his fedora and tosses it into the air. The hat miraculously lands squarely on the hook of a coatrack beside him. Without a second look he approaches the woman. Before she even sees him, he leaps up and lands upon a stool, suavely spinning into place beside her. She looks up, surprised. He gives her a smile, and without a word motions for the bartender across the way.

CLINK! Two glasses toast, and our guy and gal take a drink. Suddenly her elbow knocks her purse from the bar. He catches it midair and returns it to her side. She smiles and thanks him, telling him she's always doing things like that. He is reminded of a joke. He tells it. She laughs. They look deeply into each other's eyes.

> Suddenly his cell phone is abuzz. He answers it; it's his buddy. There's been a mix-up and he has to go. He frowns. He asks if he might call her sometime. Before he can finish his sentence she hands him a napkin with her number written in lipstick. He takes it with a smile and turns to leave. He makes his way to the coatrack and retrieves his hat. He turns back for one last look but she is gone, vanished into the night.

So there's your fully edited scene. Again, it seems to be playing just right. The pacing, the energy, the drama, everything feels great! But there's just one problem: It is WAY TOO LONG! In fact, the running time is almost DOUBLE what you've been asked to deliver.

Okay, so what do you do? How do you streamline a scene that in your eyes flows perfectly, has mood, character, and style? Well, let's revisit the original plan's logline and outline.

Plan Logline: "Guy meets gal in club and gets her number"

PLAN OUTLINE:

1. **A GUY WALKS INTO A CLUB**
2. **HE SEES A WOMAN SITTING ALONE AT THE BAR**
3. **HE APPROACHES HER AND INTRODUCES HIMSELF**
4. **HE BUYS HER A DRINK**
5. **HE CHARMS HER WITH A JOKE**
7. **HE GETS HER PHONE NUMBER**
8. **HE LEAVES**

Now that we've reviewed the outline of our plan, let's revisit the edited scene. We need to isolate those moments that may be great creative embellishments and that you may have some emotional attachment to, BUT which are not essential to the plan—and therefore not essential to the basic story you are trying to tell. Even though certain moments in your edited scene may feel like they add great character dimension and amazing content, your piece is too long. And when considered in light of the larger episode, your overlong scene could threaten to drag the show down by spending too much time on unnecessary information.

Okay, so now let's look at the scene again and underline our NON-ESSENTIAL moments:

A guy walks into a club. He looks about the room and spots a beautiful woman sitting alone at the bar. He removes his fedora and tosses it into the air. The hat miraculously lands squarely on the hook of a coatrack beside him. Without a second look he approaches the woman. Before she even sees him, he leaps up and lands upon a stool, suavely spinning into place beside her. She looks up, surprised. He smiles, and without a word motions for the bartender across the way.

CLINK! Two glasses toast, and our guy and gal take a drink. Suddenly her elbow knocks her purse from the bar. He catches it midair and returns it to her side. She smiles and thanks him, telling him she's always doing things like that. He is reminded of a joke. He tells it. She laughs. They look deeply into each other's eyes.

Suddenly, his cell phone is abuzz. He answers it; it's his buddy. There's been a mix-up and he has to go. He frowns. He asks if he might call her sometime. Before he can finish his sentence she hands him a napkin with her number written in lipstick. He takes it with a smile and turns to leave. He makes his way to the coatrack and retrieves his hat. He turns back for one last look but she is gone, vanished into the night.

As you can see, plenty of juicy details and stylistic touches can be and, in our case, need to be cut. They are unnecessary to the overall story, and because of time constraints, have to go. Now, it is not always the case that every one of these moments would have to be cut. It is always possible that your boss will agree to cut some time elsewhere in the show to save some of your golden moments, but it is important to train yourself to be able to SEE these cuts.

As an editor you must master the art of spotting the non-essential. You must always return to your basic plan and strip your scene free of its excesses. Truthfully, unless your added details are incredible, the audience (who spends most of its time trying to follow the larger story) won't even remember them.

LISTEN TO YOUR NOTES

The act of "Killing Your Babies" is by no means an easy one. Luckily, most shows have built-in safeguards to help you make the hard choices.

They are called PRODUCERS, and there is no point in the process where they can be more of an asset than when it's time to trim the fat.

When producers come into your bay to watch your cut and give you "notes" (suggested and/or demanded changes to your edit), they do not have your same emotional attachments to the footage. They did not toil and sweat to find the magic before them. They are OBJECTIVE, and that's precisely why they're there. The editing process needs that objective second set of eyes to come in and help the editor see through the fog of personal attachments.

This isn't always a pleasant experience, of course. It's a tough thing to have a stranger come into your den of creation and tell you to change what you've suffered to realize. Doesn't he know how HARD that was? Doesn't she get how WELL it's working? Doesn't he realize how FAR it's come? It's almost impossible not to be somewhat defensive and over-protective of your material, but you MUST let go of that. You need to trust the producer's objectivity, and the truth is, often this stage in the process can be one of the most educational.

The more you learn to cut, the more you learn to edit.

I can't tell you how many producers, executive producers, and network executives I have fought through the years to keep things in my scenes that, upon later reflection, really needed to go. And it is these experiences, these lost battles, that have served as my best education in self-editing. They have taught me to separate myself from my attachments and to see things more practically and objectively every step of the way. So always be sure to step back and **listen to your notes**. Digest them. Truly appreciate what they mean. Learn from them and apply that learning to your process moving forward. The more you can take from the experiences and perspectives of others about the nature of storytelling, the more efficient and effective you will become. You will start killing fewer babies and will receive fewer notes because you will instinctively be making the tough calls for yourself much earlier in the process.

Nowadays my first cuts generally end up very close to the length they need to be. At every step of the edit I weigh my choices against the big-picture objective and the basic plan I am trying to illustrate. I unconsciously kill my babies before I have time to become too attached to them. I become, in effect, my own producer.

Now don't get me wrong, this is NOT EASY. Some of these "babies" will be pretty hard to lose. The fact is, there will undoubtedly be great moments of color, character, and drama that may play beautifully in your scene but are simply not essential and ultimately have to go. With reality TV's hundreds of hours of raw material and mere minutes of screen time, there's just not enough room for all the gold.

TRIM YOUR BITES

> *"If I have a bite in my cut that runs longer than 10 seconds, there better be a very good reason."*
>
> Jackson Anderer, Editor,
> *Extreme Makeover: Home Edition* and *Celebrity Apprentice*

Streamlining is an essential skill to hone when dealing with the reality footage within a scene. It is just as critical when dealing with the INTERVIEW BITE. As we all know, some people in this world are WORDY. All you want them to do is just get to the point, but they just go ON and ON! That said, one of the most important lessons to learn when tightening a scene for time is how to **TRIM YOUR BITES**.

Interview exists to support the reality of the moment, not equal it or take its place. Too much interview will keep the audience out of the action. It will disconnect them from the world that they are meant to get lost in, so keep it short, keep it direct, and keep it simple.

In the Bay:

Here's an interview example to be trimmed:

Let's say we're cutting a scene for *Big Brother*. We are incorporating a bite wherein a contestant assesses his first day in the house, lamenting his lack of an ally.

"I'm not sure what I'm going to do here. I mean, everywhere I turn it seems like someone is out to get me. Honestly, I don't know who to trust! I don't know what to do!"

This is a fairly wordy way to say something pretty simple. So let's look at the statement again and try to identify what we can trim from it. (Cutting the underlined words should easily and nicely streamline the bite.)

"I'm not sure what I'm going to do here. I mean, everywhere I turn it seems like someone is out to get me. Honestly, I don't know who to trust! I don't know what to do!"

The new statement would play like this:

"I'm not sure what to do. Everywhere I turn someone is out to get me. I don't know who to trust!"

This is a much tighter and more succinct way to say the same thing. It is a much stronger and more focused use of your time and material. Of course, when streamlining a bite remember that your audio edits MUST be smooth. If you can't make the trims work for your ear, don't do them.

FINAL WORDS ON STREAMLINING AND TIGHTENING

As reality TV editors, our ultimate boss is the audience we seek to engage and entertain. We toil and sweat for THEM. We serve at THEIR pleasure. They trust us with their time and attention, so our responsibility is to respect that trust. This is why, at every stage of the editorial process we must ask ourselves: *Are we being efficient with our material? Are we being concise with our scene? Are we doing what's best for the story as a whole and not simply serving our emotional attachments?* In reality TV editing there is no room for excess or indulgence or ego—only strong, meaningful, succinct story. Both Leonardo da Vinci and Steve Jobs said it, so it's probably true: ***"Simplicity is the highest form of sophistication."***

CHAPTER 10 REVIEW

Choose the correct answers from the lettered list.

1. Once you have a cut that you feel confident about, it's time to do something crudely referred to as _____ ____ _____.

2. Reviewing your original _____ can be invaluable to the process of streamlining and tightening your scene.

3. Streamlining is an essential skill to hone when dealing with the reality footage. But it is just as critical when dealing with the _____ ____.

4. Your job is to deliver the best cut possible, and deliver that cut __
___.

5. In order to learn and improve as a storyteller and an editor, always
_____ __ ___ ____.

6. Luckily, most shows have built-in safeguards to help you make the
hard choices when trimming the fat. They are called _____.

   a. "To time"
   b. Listen to your notes
   c. Scene plan
   d. "Killing your babies"
   e. Producers
   f. Interview bite

Answers: 1-d, 2-c, 3-f, 4-g, 5-b, 6-e

Watch and Learn

Go grab a recorded episode of your favorite reality show, a piece of paper,
and a pen. Start from the beginning and watch through the show. As you
do, imagine you have been given the task of cutting five minutes out of it.
As you watch, note any look, line, or action that may seem interesting or
engaging but is not ESSENTIAL to the story that is being told. Now, you
may be thinking that these shows have already gone through this process
and that there couldn't possibly be anything left to cut. The truth is, no
matter how much you streamline a scene, there is always more that can
go. So get to it. Find that fat and trim the show down to size.

**The scene-building steps discussed in the preceding chapters are
depicted on the next page as a flowchart that should provide you with
a quick review and overview of the editing process.**

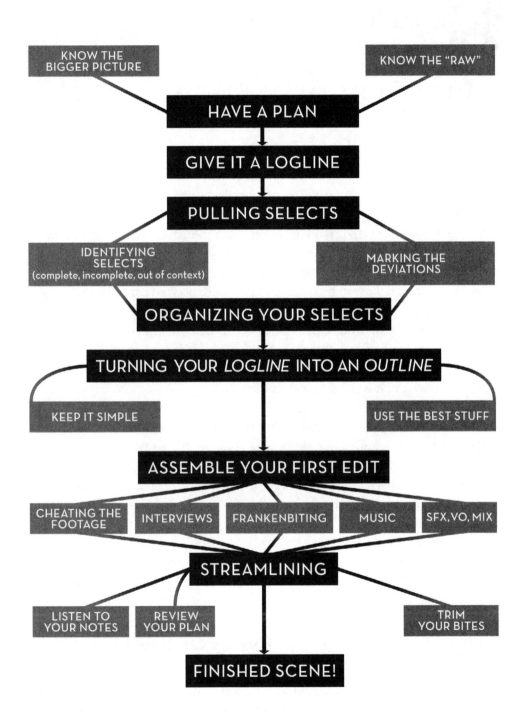

CHAPTER 11

ALL SHAPES AND SIZES

So far we've discussed the fundamentals of building a basic reality scene. But reality television can be a mercurial creature. And, in truth, it is ANYTHING but BASIC. The medium embraces a number of SUB-GENRES and SUB-GENRE HYBRIDS. And each sub-genre has different types and styles of scenes that you will be charged with building.

I'm sure you are aware that when you watch something like *American Idol* you are clearly watching a very different show stylistically than, say, *Jersey Shore*, right? Obviously there are huge differences between a show that judges singing and a show that documents drunken, 20something debauchery, and those differences are often reflected in the style of a show's editing. Certain types of scenes or sequences that might be found in one show will never be found in the other.

But whether you are cutting a scene showing the surprise reveal of a renovated house or a scene showing the arrival of a new character in a soap-opera-like reality show or a scene showing the ritualistic elimination of a contestant, the basic tools we've discussed still apply. You are still telling a story that you found in the raw footage. To breathe life into that story, you use interview bites, music, and SFX. From show to show, from sub-genre to sub-genre, only the scene's style, tone, and perhaps pacing might change. Your BASIC APPROACH to building the scene remains the same. However, as a strong reality TV editor, it is important to appreciate the field's various sub-genres and understand their inherent stylistic differences, and be prepared to deliver on them when necessary.

THREE MAJOR SUB-GENRES OF REALITY TV

Before we discuss the different types of scenes editors might be asked to cut, we should first understand the basic reality show sub-genres that they derive from. Considering the wealth of reality shows that currently

132

air, such a list can be open to a good bit of debate. That said, here are my three basic SUB-GENRES of reality TV: **Competition/Game Show**, **Docu-Soap**, and **Documentary**.

1. Competition/Game Show

This is a fairly broad sub-genre. It can cover everything from singing and dancing to dating to weight loss. The one constant, though, is contestants competing for a prize. On some shows, the contestants compete for a lavish cash prize. On others, instead of outright cash, the players vie for a choice job or a professional opportunity. Still other shows might focus on a potential romantic relationship as the prize. In these types of shows slim threads of plot are often reinforced heavily, so that viewers can easily follow the game, and character traits are bolstered to heighten STRATEGY and TENSION among the players. Usually a HOST is employed to introduce/explain the various aspects of the game and to moderate, judge, or at least check in with the competitors as they progress in the game. Some examples of popular competition/game shows are *Survivor*, *The Bachelor*, *The Amazing Race*, *American Idol*, *The Voice*, *Top Chef*, and *Big Brother*.

2. Docu-Soap

This sub-genre focuses on the day-to-day drama in the lives of a chosen few individuals. The camera is *purported* to take a "fly on the wall" perspective—merely documenting the events that unfold before it. In truth, these shows definitely have some level of direction and behind-the-scenes social orchestration mixed in with their real reality. In essence, they are *dramatically heightened* versions of reality. Docu-soap subjects often "play" themselves, with a little help from an off-camera producer who's job it is to stimulate/goad/cajole the characters a bit whenever necessary to ensure that compelling drama and conflict ensues. This sort of show often, but not always, combines straight-ahead reality scenes with supporting interviews. A few examples of the docu-soap sub-genre are *The Real Housewives* (of various cities), *Keeping Up with the Kardashians*, *Jersey Shore*, *Here Comes Honey Boo Boo*, and *Duck Dynasty*.

3. Documentary

Whereas the docu-soap *purports* to take a "fly on the wall" perspective, this one actually does. This sub-genre of show is less about sensationalism, exploitation, and exaggeration and more about documenting the facts as they ACTUALLY happened. This is not to say that punchy editing and the careful selection of what is and isn't shown don't go a very long way in creating a sense of drama and/or tension in these shows. Whether it is the basics of preparing gluten-free salty caramel cupcakes, a ride along with an inner-city cop, or a safari through the African wild, this sub-genre *celebrates* the truth—as it is carefully selected for the audience to see. Viewers tune in BECAUSE it's real. They are not interested in character arcs or plot development or prizes or eliminations. They have an interest in the topic at hand and simply want to observe it as it happens. And in the best of these shows, the truth is more entertaining than any fictionalized variation could be. Some examples are:*Anthony Bourdain: No Reservations, COPS, Antiques Roadshow,* and *The First 48.*

IMITATION WITH A TWIST (A.K.A. HYBRIDS)

I've worked in reality TV for over a decade now, and in that time I've had the opportunity to play many parts. I've obviously worked steadily as an editor, but I've also pitched, and even sold, reality shows of my own. And through the years I've found that there is one formula for pitching and selling a show that works better than any other: **Imitation with a twist**.

When a show does well, other networks want shows like it—but not *exactly* like it. They want to put their own brand or angle on it. The way they often do this is by combining sub-genres to create a HYBRID. If a non-competitive weight-loss show is doing well on VH1, NBC might create a competitive weight-loss show. If a simple renovation documentary is doing well on TLC, ABC might create a self-improvement/renovation show or a docu-soap show that follows the lives of renovators.

As a competent reality TV editor, it is important to not just appreciate the various sub-genres of the medium but also to be prepared to combine and intermingle them as each assignment requires.

SCENE TYPES AND TERMS

Along with reality TV's various sub-genres come many different styles of scene. Some are specific to one sub-genre. Some can be found in a few. And some are prevalent in all.

Below is a list of the more important scene types and scene terms that you will encounter on your travels through reality TV editing.

COLD OPEN ("PREVIOUSLY ON," SUPER TEASE): Most reality shows have what is called a **Cold Open**—a driving *montage* that comes at the very beginning of the show and previews all of the juiciest moments ahead. (Montage technique is discussed a few paragraphs later.) A cold open is like a movie trailer, albeit much shorter and more intense. The style, duration, and tone of the cold open will vary somewhat from show to show.

If you are cutting a cold open for the first episode of *Jersey Shore*, you might begin with shots of the group arriving at the shore and then montage quickly through some of the wildest and most dramatic moments of the episode. Perhaps it's the scream of an angry Snooki, who's been locked out of the house, or the tearful collapse of a devastated JWOWW who's just been dumped by her boyfriend. It might be a lively Ronnie swinging a fist at a cop. One after another, these moments will fly by above a series of dramatic, driving music cues. Generally, your shot sequence will build as your music cues build, finally reaching a crescendo with a brief glimpse at the episode's best or most anticipated moment. Perhaps a drunken Pauly D passes out cold on the dance floor as The Situation yells for 911!

Sometimes this opening sequence will focus on events from previous episodes. (This approach is common on competition shows, where the audience needs to get caught up on the game.) In these instances this opening sequence would be referred to as a **Previously On**. At other times, when introducing the first episode of the series, it will include not just what's to come in the episode, but also clips of what is to come throughout the entire season. This is referred to as a **Super Tease**.

TEASE: The **Tease** is similar in concept to the cold open, but on a much smaller scale. It will traditionally come at the end of every act and offer a sneak peek at what's in store after the commercial break. The differences between a **Tease** and a cold open are length and content. Whereas a cold open might run a minute or more, a **Tease** is usually no longer than fifteen seconds. The tease will also often stick to only the content in the immediately upcoming act.

ACT OUT: The **Act Out** refers to the last few moments of the act before you cut to your tease and/or commercial break. The idea here is to find the most tantalizing "cliff-hanging" moment you can, and then dial up its anticipation to the max. A classic example is the judges' deliberation before the elimination of a contestant. Here you would cut from desperate face to desperate face as the music builds to the absolute boiling point. Then, just before the judges reveal their decision, you cut to a commercial. You want to bring your viewers to the brink, then cut out and leave them begging to see what's next.

MONTAGE: This is a basic editing technique that you will find in any show you work on. Technically, the cold open and the tease are examples of it, but I am describing it here as it pertains to work within a scene. The **Montage** is essentially the juxtaposition of clips, cut together, scored with music, and sometimes bridged with unifying bites. A montage is often used to condense time. In just a few minutes or less, it might show bits and pieces of real-life activities that lasted hours, days, even weeks. Instead of playing such lengthy activities out in full, you select only the most significant moments and cut them back-to-back as a sort of highlights reel. Think of the famous shopping spree montage in the film *Pretty Woman,* or the signature training sequences from the *Rocky* films.

A great reality TV montage example might be a *challenge prep scene* from a competition show like *Hell's Kitchen.* Ordinarily there is not enough time to follow the different competing chefs preparing every step of their various dishes. Instead, you might create a montage focusing solely on the most colorful, engaging, and narrative-appropriate moments. You would then score it with tense music and perhaps mix in a few interview bites from different characters expressing their anticipation.

Another popular use of the montage is found in renovation or home makeover shows. Let's face it, no one REALLY wants to sit through three days of hammering, sanding, and painting. Your viewers want to see how the project started and how it ended up. They want to marvel at dramatic transformations without having to suffer the minutiae of the work that went into them. That said, viewers do want to know that work was done, even if they only have the patience to endure a taste of it. In this instance, a montage is invaluable. It allows you to move quickly through the process of renovation, highlighting only choice moments. This way, the audience can appreciate three days of work in just a few minutes.

BACKGROUND PACKAGE: A popular first episode staple in many reality TV shows is a group of "scene-lets" called **Background Packages**. These are basically mini-montages that serve to quickly introduce each member of a show's cast, highlighting the qualities that will make a particular character memorable, as well as hinting at personal stakes and underlying motivations. Often they will include interview bites from the individuals and their family and friends, mixed with footage of their lives at home. They may even include footage of a character traveling to, and arriving at, the show's location. Generally, background packages should run no longer than a minute, usually less.

HOUSE REALITY: The **House Reality** scene is an important fixture in many shows, especially competitions. (By HOUSE I mean the place where the competitors will live or commune when not in play— e.g., *Survivor*'s campsite, *Hell's Kitchen*'s dormitory, any dating show's contestant living quarters, etc.) Such a scene, shot at the "house," might cover first episode arrivals, mid-episode downtime, pre-challenge anticipations, or post-elimination fallout. Sometimes the scene is captured by live cameras and sometimes by the space's fixed "spy" cameras that roll unmanned 24/7. Within these scenes you will build many of the relationships, animosities, alliances, and betrayals between your characters. This is where we truly get to know the many personalities and develop the personal side of the story.

THE CHALLENGE REVEAL CEREMONY: A staple of the competition/game show sub-genre is the **Challenge Reveal Ceremony**. Before a game can begin, the players AND the audience need to know WHAT THAT GAME IS. Often the competitors will be summoned to a special location for the challenge reveal ceremony scene, which will normally be led by the show's host, who is sometimes also its judge. The audience will learn, along with the contestants, what the episode's next challenge will be, how it works, and its underlying purpose within the show. In general, the challenge reveal ceremony will be *blocked* (a term that refers to a scene's choreography between cameras and cast) and shot more formally than your average reality scene. Players will respectfully line up and face their host, listening obediently. It is, after all, a ceremony! Also, such a scene is usually shot with a multi-cam setup (more than one camera shooting the same material simultaneously), which will give the whole experience the slicker feel of higher production values.

The goal when editing a challenge reveal ceremony is to build as much suspense and anticipation as possible. Often you will hold back as long as you can on various announcements and pronouncements, instead lingering on the arrival of the players, their wait for the host, and then the host's arrival. To build the most tension, you will want to choose your many close-up reaction shots and reaction interview bites carefully. The competitors need to literally hang on every word from their host. The viewers need to feel the contestants' anticipation in every frame. Only once you can cut that anticipation with a knife should you then climax with the host's announcement of the game.

THE ELIMINATION CHALLENGE: The **Elimination Challenge** is the centerpiece of many competition reality shows. It is the episode's main game, race, or test of skill. This is what the show has been building toward, and its outcome will often determine the fate of the competitors.

Normally these scenes will begin at a slow, fairly continuous pace, and gradually build to a pulse-pounding montage of activity. Some like to call this kind of scene the TICKING CLOCK SCENE. Imagine a ticking clock at the bottom of the screen, but not your average, everyday clock. This is a clock that actually goes faster and faster as more time passes. What might seem to start out as a depiction of real time is, by the end, a clock spinning wildly out of control.

Whether your **elimination challenge** scene has contestants competing on an action-packed obstacle course or enduring the preparation of a tricky five-star dish, the approach is the same: Use your elements to slowly and purposefully move from calm to chaos. And, just as in any televised race, what starts out covering ALL of the players will slowly and deliberately zero in on only the TRUE contenders. However, unlike other televised races, this is not LIVE. It is orchestrated and manipulated after the fact, so you can alter its pace to accelerate the tension. You can make it look like a much closer race than it truly was. You can play up setbacks with great drama and ramp up the contestants' emotions far beyond what they might have been.

THE ELIMINATION CEREMONY: In some reality competition shows, such as *The Amazing Race*, the challenge scenes end with a clear winner: Whoever gets there first wins. In other shows, especially on programs where contestants are observed and subjectively judged (*Hell's Kitchen, America's Next Top Model, The Apprentice*), the ultimate winner might be left in question until the very end of the episode. The judge(s) may need to discuss or deliberate on the outcome before making a decision, which they will eventually reveal in a formal **Elimination Ceremony** scene.

In this sort of scene, the competitors will often gather in a formal line, and the host and/or judge(s) will preside over them. One by one the players will be addressed, at which point they may be interrogated about their performance. Some competitors may gloat; some may desperately apologize and beg to stay, while others may attempt to aggressively defend their missteps. In the end, the judgment will be revealed and at least one contestant will be sent packing.

For most elimination ceremonies, facial close-ups, tense cutting, and the building of pulse-pounding anticipation are the names of the game. The primary stylistic difference between this and the previously mentioned challenge reveal ceremony is the volume of the drama. If you were at a drama level 10 in the challenge reveal, take the elimination to 30! Here you officially have the license to go ALL the way to over-the-top melodrama. This would be the time to swoop in on faces, swell your cymbals, and smash your dramatic percussion hits. Before names are called by judges, you will stretch out the anticipation by building overlong desperate pauses. The judge may say, "And the loser is...," and with this you would cut to an anxious player's face, then back to a judge, then to another player's face, then back to the judge, and so on. Stretch it out as long as you can. This may sound like *too* much of a good thing, but in the world of competition reality, it is expected. The ultimate crescendo, of course, is the revelation of which contestant will be going home. This is followed by the classic reality convention known as THE WALK OF SHAME.

THE WALK OF SHAME: The last beat of many competition reality shows is **The Walk of Shame**. This is an emotionally charged sequence that uses footage of the eliminated contestant(s) leaving the game. The remaining players look on as the loser, in interview bites, talks about how much it sucks to lose. If you can fit a few close-up tears in there, it's always a plus.

DIFFERENT, BUT THE SAME

I'm not going to lie: No two reality shows are ever exactly the same. Every network wants its show to be different. Networks want each of their competition/game shows and each of their docu-soaps to have its own identifiable freshness. For instance, one show might rely heavily on interview bites and narration, while another tries to keep to mostly real-time reality. One show might use every whiz-bang flashy effect available to them, while another may go with strictly simple cuts and dissolves. But as much as they want to change things up and stand out from the pack, there are certain conventions they would never veer from. There is a *language* to the dating show and to the renovation show and certain *types* of scenes and sequences the audience expects to see in each. Knowing these fundamental types of scenes, understanding these most established of reality conventions, is crucial to getting the editing job and doing it right. You can't play in the game if you don't know the rules. Even more importantly, you can't BREAK the rules if you don't know what rules there are to break.

CHAPTER 11 REVIEW

Choose the correct answers from the lettered list.

1. A _____ _____ scene is one that covers moments of non-competition throughout the series.

2. A popular first episode staple in many reality TV shows is a group of smaller "scene-lets" called _____ _____.

3. What do you call the main game, race, or test of skill that a competition show builds to, the outcome of which will often determine the fate of the competitors?

4. The _____ is a "fly on the wall" style of show. The cameras are purported to be purely observational in this style of show, which is probably the closest to true documentary.

5. *Survivor, The Amazing Race,* and *Big Brother* are all examples of what kind of reality show?

6. What do you call the montage that comes at the very beginning of the show and is meant to preview all of the juiciest moments ahead?

7. If one sub-genre of reality show is combined with another, you have what is called a _____ reality show.

   a. Background packages
   b. Hybrid
   c. The competition/game show
   d. House reality
   e. The elimination challenge
   f. Docu-soap
   g. Cold open

Answers: 1-d, 2-a, 3-e, 4-f, 5-c, 6-g 7-b

WATCH AND LEARN

Go grab a pen and a piece of paper, and fire up the Web. Find your local TV listings (http://www.tvguide.com/ should suffice). Once there, scan every station and program over a two-week period and pick out any reality show you can find. As you find them, write down their names. Try to find at least ten, preferably more. Once finished, go through your list, show by show, and next to each one write the sub-genre it most closely resembles. If it's a hybrid, then write the multiple sub-genres it most closely resembles.

CHAPTER 12

HOMEWORK

It took me a long time to embrace the value of homework. I have always been a bit of a TV addict, and I'd be lying if I said I wasn't a master at the art of procrastination. So, homework and I were not what you would call fast friends. I only really began to embrace the concept when I started dipping my toes into the waters of theater and acting. This was the one place where being unprepared could spell ACTUAL humiliation. I mean, you're stepping out in front of a live audience. You NEED to know your lines. You HAVE to know your blocking. And it wouldn't hurt to be GOOD! Almost overnight I was forced to change my ways. I quickly went from Mr. Mañana to Mr. No-Time-like-the-Present.

I was suddenly spending hours reading, memorizing, and rehearsing. And each and every day I would step into school and up on that stage experiencing something I never had before—CONFIDENCE in my work. And this was not just any confidence; it was that very special confidence that comes from knowing deep down that you are truly prepared.

In reality TV editing, homework and preparation are absolutely essential. You never know when your opportunity to move up and get ahead will present itself. Tests can come in the most surprising and unpredictable ways, and you need that same confidence that I had stepping on that stage. You need to not just believe; you need to absolutely KNOW that you are prepared.

ONCE AGAIN, WATCH AND LEARN

I have now spent more than 100 pages laying out the various skills, tricks, rules, and tools of reality TV editing. We have discussed finding and structuring a reality story. We have covered manipulating the raw and cheating. We have touched upon the various elements that combine with your footage to help tell your story, and in our last chapter we covered many different types of shows and styles of scene you may encounter.

What's next? Well, now that you have a solid CONCEPTUAL handle on this stuff, it's time to get a PRACTICAL one, and the first step in getting practical is research. So, as I've challenged you to do in the many chapter exercises throughout this book, it's time, once again, to **Watch and Learn**.

> *"I honestly suggest you watch everything you can. I don't care if you love the show or hate it. Watch it. That's how you learn."*
>
> Tim Roche, Editor,
> *It's Always Sunny in Philadelphia* and *Undercover Boss*

TiVo, Hulu, iTunes, Netflix—even just plain old TV—should now be your best friends. You need to start tuning in on a regular basis and *analyzing* what you see. Start watching from the perspective of the editor who puts it all together. Think about the various techniques and tricks that have been covered in this book. Try to spot the cheats. See how music cues change from moment to moment, scene to scene. Do they properly accentuate the drama? Do they feel well placed and well chosen? Assess how the interview bites, SFX, and VO are used. See for yourself how these tools really do elevate the viewing experience. And try to identify the mistakes you'll find as well. Not all reality shows are well cut, but that doesn't mean you can't learn from them just the same. Where do things fall flat and why? What might *you* have done differently?

The truth is, right now, with what we've covered in this book, you already possess knowledge and perspective that many WORKING editors do not. You are thinking about things THE RIGHT WAY, and that is huge! That's something that too many editors out there just do not do. In fact, many of them are so set in their ways that they never will think about things in the right way. If you can apply this little book's knowledge and reinforce it with research and study of everything on the tube, you will be well on your way to leaving many of even the most seasoned editors in the dust.

Quick Tip: Pre-Job Recon

At-home viewing and research is an invaluable part of the learning experience every step of the way. But it is never more essential than just before you are about to start a new job.

If your gig starts on a Monday, you'll want to spend the previous Saturday and Sunday familiarizing yourself with what you're stepping into. You need to know the show's basic style and format. You need to see examples of how other editors have done it. You need to see what a polished and finished episode looks like. After all, you are about to be paid a lot of money to do it for yourself. So, it might be a good idea to have some sense of exactly HOW it's done, right?

The best-case scenario is that the show you are about to work on already has episodes in the can. Perhaps you are coming in mid-season, or even into a second or third season. If this is the case, simply ask your new employers for a DVD or two or find the show on iTunes. As you watch any and all episodes you can get, take note of the pacing, the musical choices, and specific styles of scene. How much does the show use interview bites? What kind of bites do they favor? What is the overall tone of the show, and how is that tone reinforced? Analyzing the actual show you are about to cut, and getting a handle on its style and structure, will give you a big head start.

Of course, you won't always be so lucky. If you are starting on a brand-new show with no finished episodes, talk to your new employers. Ask them to recommend some similar shows to watch. They may give you other stuff the company has produced, or they may give you shows within the same genre as what you are about to cut. If it's a docu-soap about bitchy rich ex-wives, they may tell you to check out *The Real Housewives*. If it is a network singing competition, they may steer you toward *American Idol* or *The Voice*. Often the next best thing is just as good as the real thing, especially if your new employer tells you so.

GET HANDS-ON

I have stressed again and again throughout this book the importance of practice. I can give you the rules of the road. I can pass on the tips and tools of the trade. But great editing comes from...well, quite simply, EDITING! The more problems you solve, the more problems you will be ABLE to solve. Not to mention that you never know when, or how, your shot will come. And when it does come, you want to be ready.

I recommend getting a non-linear editing program that you can use on your home computer. Avid and Final Cut-pro have relatively *affordable* program packages. I have both on my laptop and use them regularly. The Avid Media Composer package is especially valuable since it is the industry standard and most likely what you will be working with on the job. I think it runs around $2,500 right now but is less than $500 if you are a student with a valid ID. (Although they aren't *super*-cheap, they're well worth your investment—trust me.) If need be, get together and pool resources with your peers. There is no substitute for hands-on practice, and the affordability and access to professional-level software available today allows you this opportunity like never before.

Note that these programs have certain hardware requirements, so be sure to research what you're buying. Be sure to find something that works with YOUR computer and YOUR hard drives. Ask questions. Check the specs.

GIVE YOURSELF A PROJECT

Here's a little secret: It is far easier to learn a computer program when you are actually making something you'd like to see finished. I learned the Avid Media Composer by making a short film in college. I was passionate about the film. I wrote the script, directed it, and couldn't wait to see it finished. This enthusiasm helped push me through some of the tougher learning curves and kept me motivated to the end. So grab a video camera and go shoot something you'd like to put together. Or volunteer to cut a wedding video. Or gather your family's home movies and design a creative compilation video. Set yourself up with a small project and commit to finishing it. Make it something that you can get excited about. This motivation will really help get you through the technical learning curve. Before you know it you'll be a master of the non-linear domain.

OTHER RESOURCES

Another great thing about getting your own editing system is that it comes with a dense and informative MANUAL. Dive into it. Absorb everything it has to say. Start teaching yourself editing shortcuts and keyboard commands. One of the best pieces of technical editing advice I ever received was "USE THE KEYBOARD, NOT THE MOUSE." Think of it as typing (which you should anyway, since you're a WRITER). Refer to the manual when you have questions. Challenge yourself to master each step in the editorial process—from ingesting the media to organizing it, cutting it, finishing it, and outputting it.

Once you've exhausted the manual, another great asset for at-home editing education is the World Wide Web and its numerous user groups and chat rooms. Some require membership, but most don't. If you have questions you can simply post them on one of these user group sites, where much more experienced editors often will provide you with quick answers.

FINAL WORDS ON HOMEWORK

Homework in reality TV editing is crucial, especially when you are trying to break in and move up. It allows you to truly study, absorb, and begin to master the craft on your own time. You can learn the technical skills required to climb the ladder and endure difficult learning curves at your own pace and in your own space. Believe me, you're going to make mistakes; we all do. Wouldn't it be preferable to make the more elementary and embarrassing ones away from the judgment of prying professional eyes? So don't wait. Get out there. Get editing. And start mastering the craft that will bring you success, wealth, and a creative career that will be the envy of all your friends.

PART 2
THE JOB

INTRODUCTION

THE BEST-KEPT JOB SECRET IN HOLLYWOOD

"Here's how I compare reality to scripted [TV] in terms of getting a job: It's simple. Think about how many hours of scripted are made a year. Now think about how many hours of reality are made a year. Honestly, there's no contest."

Jackson Anderer, Editor,
Extreme Makeover: Home Edition and *Celebrity Apprentice*

At this point we've covered the basics of how to build a strong reality scene from start to finish. We've reinforced the importance of the plan. We've celebrated the art of the cheat. We've examined the many uses for the interview bite, including the power of the Frankenbite. We've talked about music, SFX, voice-over and the mix. We have covered every key step necessary to delivering top-notch edits quickly and efficiently. So what's next? Well, now that you have the skills, it's time to find the audience. It's time to put your tools to the test.

It's time to get a JOB!

I introduced this book by calling the job of a reality TV editor *"the easily accessible, high-paying Hollywood job that nobody knows about."* I asserted that it is *"the best-kept SHOWBIZ JOB SECRET around."* I stand by these statements. Reality television is exploding and expanding every day. More and more jobs are being created because more and more networks are choosing to produce reality. From a network's budgetary viewpoint, the price is right: There are no writers or actors to overpay. There are no fancy cameras with truckloads of lighting and grip gear, and most reality is non-union, which means major savings across the board. Add to that the fact that reality often matches and even beats scripted TV in the ratings (*American Idol*, anyone?), and I think it's pretty obvious that the genre is here to stay. It's simply less fiscal risk for the same return.

What does this mean for you?

Well, in reality TV, the most essential craftsman is the editor. A producer can come up with an idea, a crew can capture that idea, but the EDITOR is the only one who can actually REALIZE that idea on the screen. Remember, the reality TV editor is equivalent to scripted television's WRITER. He or she is the one finding, shaping, and expressing the story. And, just liked writers in scripted TV, it is very hard to do with just one or two. Often you need an entire team to get the job done right. I've worked on shows that have had as many as 15 or 20 editors working night and day to turn a show around quickly and get it on the air. Bottom line, lots of reality shows, all of which need lots and lots of editors, means many opportunities for you to make lots and lots of money! It also means that when starting out, you can move through the ranks quickly because you're in demand.

I have never been on staff at any production company. Most of my jobs last no longer than three or four months. And yet in 10 years, I have never struggled to find a job, and my rate just keeps going up. It is an editor's market out there. It is YOUR market. There are quite simply more jobs than there are solid editors to fill them. They NEED you. They want to hire you. You just have to know how to help them do that.

So how is it done? How do you move through these so-called ranks so quickly? What are the steps to such alluring success? Well, there are quite a few. And in the following chapters I will lay them out. I will organize them into "stages." Each stage will deal with a different set of steps on your stairway to professional success. And if you follow these steps correctly, your chances of moving up quickly, making big TV shows, and even bigger bucks are VERY, VERY high.

CHAPTER 13

GETTING IN

"Before I broke into television, I'd ask everyone I could think of: 'How did you get into the business?' Almost every answer started with, 'Well, I didn't get started in the usual way.' I quickly learned that there is no standard way to break in. The best thing is to speak to everyone you know about your desire and network, network, network. It may take a while, but unless people know your desire to work in this business, you'll never be invited to apply for a job."

Aaron Simard, Producer,
E! True Hollywood Story

Before you can start climbing the Hollywood ladder, you first have to actually GET INTO Hollywood. So our first stage is all about GETTING IN THE DOOR. Right now you are an outsider with ambition. What you want to be is an insider putting that ambition to good use. As Al Pacino says in the mob film *Donnie Brasco*, you want to be *"a friend of ours."* And here's how it's done.

STEP 1: THE RÉSUMÉ

You may be skeptical about your need for a résumé at this point. After all, you haven't worked in entertainment, so how can you possibly have an ENTERTAINMENT résumé? The reality is that EVERYONE must have a résumé. Companies are going to ask for it, and when they do, you had better be prepared with something intelligible and professional to present.

A résumé can make or break an employment opportunity. Prospective employers want to know that you think ahead and are prepared. They want to see that you are a professional who will treat the job seriously. They want to see that you can express yourself clearly on paper. This is vital to their assessment of whether you're worth their time. Also, in lieu of a card, the résumé is the premier "leave behind." It is the prospective employer's quick and easy resource for discussing you with others and contacting you after the fact.

So what can you put on your entertainment résumé if you have no entertainment experience? There's an old saying: *"Dress for the job you want, not the job you have."* What this means is that you should carry yourself the way you want other people to perceive you. Take control of your professional future and tell the world around you where you're headed and when; don't wait for them to tell you. The same is true of crafting your first entertainment résumé. You may not have loads of TV credits to fill your page, but you do have experiences, and from these experiences you have developed skills. You just need to present these skills with an eye toward working in entertainment.

The tacit understanding behind your résumé page's listings MUST ALWAYS BE that each and everything you've done up to this point has been intended to prepare you for the job you are now attempting to win. Sure you may have been brewing lattes for yuppies, but what you were REALLY DOING was strengthening your people skills and learning to deliver on time—two talents every Hollywood job requires. Sure you may have been working phones and keeping files for your uncle the realtor, but what you were REALLY DOING was multitasking and managing the unexpected by thinking on your feet—skills that have SHOW BUSINESS written all over them. By simply reframing the way in which you present yourself, you can turn most any working experience into a calculated step towards your entertainment career.

The first thing you want to put on your résumé is your name and contact info. It should go right at the top, centered, in a large bold, professional-looking (no wild curlicues) font. Remember, if they like you, you'll want to make it as easy as possible for them to contact you. After that it's time to start making lists.

A résumé is basically a series of lists. Each list will touch upon a different strength you possess, and within each list should be any pertinent details that say, "I'm the ideal choice to fill your position."

The first list (depending on the résumé guide you're following) should cover your education. Are you a high school graduate? Where did you go to school? Did you win any awards or take part in any extracurricular activities? How do these awards and activities relate to the job you are pursuing? Are you a college graduate or are you currently in college? What is your focus or major?

The next list should cover your employment experiences. Remember, even if you haven't worked in the entertainment industry, it's quite possible the basic skills you've developed in past jobs will be the same ones utilized in your first Hollywood job. Imagine what those skills would be and highlight them. For an entry-level Hollywood job I would focus on your people skills, organizational skills, quick-thinking and problem-solving prowess, your ability to remain calm under pressure, etc. (And be prepared to discuss these skills in detail in an interview.) Try to give each of your previous jobs an official title. This reinforces the fact that you're a professional and that you take employment seriously. If you worked as a temp, answering phones and making photocopies somewhere, call your position Clerical Assistant. Don't exaggerate your previous experiences, but don't underplay them either.

Finally, list any and all SPECIAL SKILLS you possess that might aid and/or play a role in the job you are seeking. Can you type? How fast? What sorts of computer programs can you use? Do you know Photoshop, Excel, Avid, or Final Cut Pro? Are you computer literate with both Mac and PC? Don't be shy. If you think it applies, write it down.

STEP 2: FINDING AN INTERNSHIP

The internship is the most common way into the entertainment industry. It's how I, and most of my peers, started out. The internship is a centuries-old tradition that stems from the concept of the apprenticeship. Throughout time, parents have offered their children to craftsmen as free labor in return for an on-the-job education. The deal was, "You can employ my child for no money if you agree to teach him your business and prepare him for gainful employment once the period of apprenticeship is complete." A Hollywood internship follows very much the same construct, with one major difference: In most Hollywood internships, it is up to the intern, NOT the boss, to navigate the trajectory of his/her own career. As an intern you will meet all sorts of people doing all kinds of jobs, and it is up to you to find the specific niche that interests you the most. The Hollywood internship lets you in the door. But then it's up to YOU to find your direction.

So how do you get an internship? Well, the easiest way is through a personal contact. This is generally a relative or friend who's already on the inside and willing to hook you up. Maybe your buddy's uncle is an agent, or your brother-in-law is a producer. Another great way in is through a college or university internship program. Many universities have these types of programs, and even if they don't already have entertainment company contacts, going through such a program can really help speed the process of landing a position. Unfortunately, most people don't have these kinds of contacts and aids, so they must work a little harder to find openings. But have no fear. Getting an internship isn't THAT hard. After all, you are basically offering to work for nothing.

So you have no personal hookups or collegiate aids. You're on your own. What do you do? Where do you go? How do you find these elusive internships and start preparing for this great high-paying creative job you've spent the last 100-plus pages reading about? Well, throw on that raincoat and fedora. It's time for a little something called DETECTIVE WORK.

Recon

The first thing you need if you want to be a proper detective is a notebook in which you'll compile all the valuable pieces of information you uncover. You are searching for clues. You are compiling information that you don't want to forget. Get a notebook. Get a pen. Write it down.

Now, fire up your computer and hop on the Internet. (You're lucky. When I started out I didn't have the World Wide Web at my fingertips. I had to conduct my investigation using trade publications and production guides, and these weren't the easiest of resources for a young New Jersey suburbanite to find.) With a few choice word searches you can get all of the information you need, and you can do it all in one sitting.

Type the words REALITY TV SHOWS into your search engine and press Enter. What you're seeking is a list of all reality TV shows currently airing in the United States. You'll quickly discover there are plenty of resources out there. Wikipedia has a pretty good rundown. You can also try realitytvworld.com and tv.com. Once you find what seems to be the most comprehensive list, copy the name of each and every show into your notebook in a column, one after the other. I know it's labor intensive, but, trust me, it's worth it.

Next, determine the production company that is behind each show on your list and jot it down next to the show's name. This step is vital to your investigation, as you will target these companies for your internship. Finding which companies produce which shows should also be a fairly easy endeavor: A simple search should suffice, but if you come up short, try IMBD.com or its subscription counterpart, IMDBpro.com. If all else fails, record the show in question, roll to the end of the credits, and look for the production company's logo. Most shows have them, and they will usually pop up as one of the very last items in the end credits. When you're done with this step there should be a company listed next to every show on your list.

On the next page is an example of the sort of list of reality shows and their production companies that you should draw up.

REALITY SHOWS AND THEIR PRODUCTION COMPANIES

AMERICA'S GOT TALENT — FREEMANTLE MEDIA

AMERICA'S NEXT TOP MODEL — ~~KEN MARK~~   10X10 ENTERTAINMENT

AMERICAN IDOL — FREEMANTLE MEDIA

AMERICAN PICKERS — CINEFLIX MEDIA

ACE OF CAKES — AUTHENTIC ENTERTAINMENT

THE BACHELOR — NEXT ENTERTAINMENT

BIG BROTHER — ENDEMOL USA

BLACK GOLD — ORIGINAL PRODUCTION

CELEBRITY APPRENTICE — MARK BURNETT PRODUCTIONS

DANCE MOM'S — COLLINS AVE PRODUCTIONS

DANCING WITH THE STARS — BBC WORLDWIDE

DEADLIEST CATCH — ORIGINAL PRODUCTIONS

DUCK DYNASTY — GURNEY PRODUCTIONS

EXTREME MAKEOVER : HOME EDITION — ENDEMOL USA

FLIPPING OUT — AUTHENTIC ENTERTAINMENT

HERE COMES HONEY BOO BOO — AUTHENTIC ENTERTAINMENT

ICE ROAD TRUCKERS — ORIGINAL PRODUCTIONS

~~JERSEY SHORE~~

JERSEYLICIOUS — ENDEMOL USA

PAWN STARS — LEFTFIELD PICTURES

THE REAL HOUSEWIVES OF BEVERLY HILLS — EVOLUTION MEDIA

THE REAL HOUSEWIVES OF NEW JERSEY — SIRENS MEDIA

THE REAL HOUSEWIVES OF NEW YORK CITY — SHED MEDIA

TODDLERS AND TIARAS — AUTHENTIC ENTERTAINMENT

SHARK TANK — MARK BURNETT PRODUCTIONS

STORAGE WARS — ORIGINAL PRODUCTIONS

SURVIVOR — MARK BURNETT PRODUCTIONS

THE VOICE — MARK BURNETT PRODUCTIONS

WIPEOUT — ENDEMOL USA

THE X-FACTOR — FREEMANTLE MEDIA

Now study your list and identify those production company names that pop up most frequently. Among these production entities are big guys and little guys. When you are trying to establish yourself and move up the Hollywood ladder it's generally better to be with the big guys (i.e., the ones making the most shows). Companies like Endemol USA and Original Productions have had loads of shows on the air, including *Big Brother*, *Wipeout*, *Ice Road Truckers*, *Deadliest Catch*, *Ax Men*, etc. The more productions a company has going, the more people they need to work on them. Also, the more series a company has on air, the more they will probably have in the future. Big companies with years of success are generally the ones that networks want to commission for new shows, so the bigger and more prolific the company, the better for you and your goal of moving IN and moving UP.

Next, turn to a fresh notebook page and make a new list. This time I want you to list the top ten to fifteen most-prolific production companies you've found. And below each company's name, write down its contact info. WAIT A MINUTE! We don't have contact info yet, do we?

The easiest way to get a production company's info is via its website. Most companies have websites, and listed on those sites are contact phone numbers, as well as email addresses and fax numbers, and even street addresses. Write all that information down.

Now root out any other pertinent information that might be available about the company. The more educated you are about a company, the more eager and qualified you will appear in your interview. Try to find out when it was started. Who started it? What are or have been its biggest hits? Who are its key personnel? Where did they come from? How did they get where they are? (I told you this was detective work.) Remember, the more you know about them, the more impressed they will be with you.

On the next page are examples of a few pages from the sort of list of production companies and their contact information that you should put together.

MOST PROLIFIC PRODUCTION COMPANIES

(* NOTE: This information is for illustration purposes only. Production companies are known to change up their contact info, periodically, especially their location. So please do your own "recon" and get your own info to be sure you're on the right track.)

ENDEMOL USA
9255 SUNSET BOULEVARD
WEST HOLLYWOOD, CA 90069
PHONE: (310) 860-9914
www.endemolusa.tv
productions — BIG BROTHER, EXTREME MAKEOVE
JERSEYLICIOUS, WIPE OUT

FREEMANTLE MEDIA
4000 WEST ALAMEDA AVENUE, 3RD FL.
BURBANK, CA 91505
PHONE: (818) 748-1100
www.FREEMANTLEMEDIA.COM
productions: AMERICAN IDOL, AMERICA'S HOT TALENT,
THE X-FACTOR

PRODUCTION COMPANIES CONTINUED...

MARK BURNETT PRODUCTIONS
3000 OLYMPIC BLVD.
SANTA MONICA, CA 90404
PHONE: (310) 903-5400
FAX: (310) 903-5566
productions — CELEBRITY APPRENTICE, SURVIVOR,
THE VOICE

ORIGINAL PRODUCTIONS
308 W. VERDUGO AVE
BURBANK, CA 91502
PHONE: (818) 295-6966
www.ORIGPROD.COM
productions — AX MEN, BLACK GOLD, DEADLIEST CATCH,
ICE ROAD TRUCKERS, STORAGE WARS

AUTHENTIC ENTERTAINMENT
2860 N. NAOMI ST.
BURBANK, CA 91504
PHONE: (323) 644-6144
productions: ACE OF CAKES, HERE COMES HONEY BOO BOO,
FLIPPING OUT, TODDLERS & TIARAS.

All right, you now have a PRODUCTION COMPANY MASTER LIST. You've categorized the top reality production houses in town. You've listed their various shows. You have noted their contact information and you have gleaned any extra info you could find about them. Now you are ready for the next step in the process: MAKING CONTACT!

Quick Tip: Collaboration

All movie and TV production is dependent upon COLLABORATION. It takes a whole team of people working together to get something up on the screen, but collaboration doesn't only apply to the ART of show business. It can and should also be a part of the art of GETTING INTO show business.

There are A LOT of people who want to work in entertainment. It's becoming more and more popular every day. It's basically getting paid for having fun! Who wouldn't want to go and be creative all day and get paid handsomely for it? So yes, a lot of people want in. And the best thing you can do for yourself is not to beat them out for the job but to JOIN them and work WITH them to FIND the jobs.

Talk with your friends. Spread the word through your social circles. Team up with others. Confer on what you've collectively learned about getting into the biz. Discuss the many questions you each have. One of the most important elements of success in any industry—and most certainly in entertainment—is CONTACTS.

IT'S ALL ABOUT WHO YOU KNOW!

The moment you start making contacts is the moment your career has officially begun. So, if you can find like-minded individuals with the same Hollywood ambitions, RIGHT OUT OF THE GATE you have made your first contacts and are already ahead of the game.

STEP 3: THE COLD CALL

"I'd say do it earlier in the morning. It sucks to spend the whole day procrastinating, only to make the cold call at 4 p.m. and get nobody there. Not only do I feel a lack of accomplishment, I let the dread of making the call hang over me the whole day. If I suck it up and call first thing, the dread lifts and I get positive fuel for the rest of the day."

Brent Kinetz, Writer/Producer

The cold call can be intimidating. It can be daunting, but it is a crucial step in landing any kind of internship. It's never an easy thing to call a stranger, out of the blue, and ask him or her to give you something. But EVERYONE DOES IT. Production companies are used to it. And when it pans out in getting you an internship, it feels fantastic. So don't be intimidated: Keep in mind that what you're asking them to give is pretty low-risk on their part. I mean, YOU are the one who is actually doing the giving. You're saying, "I will be your slave if you teach me stuff." You're asking them to let you do things for THEM for FREE! That's really not something they would be offended by or irritated to hear. Lastly, remember that everything is easier the more you do it. It's just like dating or exercise: The first time is tough, the second a little better, and eventually it's a snap. So take a deep breath, stay focused, and start dialing.

Cold Calling Tips

A few pointers when it comes to the COLD CALL: Speak clearly. Be respectful and friendly, while at the same time direct and to the point. Choose your questions carefully. Keep them simple, but COVER your bases. Even if you are turned down you can still benefit by asking pointed questions that will provide you with valuable information.

Below are a few examples:

- *"If you're not looking for an intern now, do you know anyone who is?"*

- *"Is there a particular department or employee to whom I should direct future inquiries?"*

- *"What duties are your interns expected perform?"*

- *"Do you guys post your own shows?"* (You obviously want to home in on companies that do their own postproduction. The easiest way to move ahead is to be promoted internally. The good news is, most companies do indeed post their own stuff.)

- *"Are there any resources you might suggest for finding reality TV internships elsewhere?"* (There are sometimes internal industry emails that list internships and other production-related jobs, but you must be referred or invited into them, so it never hurts to ask.)

- *"Could I email you my résumé for your files?"* (If they say yes, great, you can then follow up with them at a later date and begin to develop an identity with the company.)

And most importantly...

- *"What is your name?"* (The moment you get someone's name, you've been introduced. That individual is now a contact. The next time you call, use his or her name, and remind this new contact of your name. He or she will immediately start to see you in a more personal light.)

If it helps, write your questions down and have them on hand for easy reference during your cold call. Your time will be limited, so you'll want to make the most of it. Besides, having a pen and paper handy is a good idea anyway. You are about to be flooded with gobs of valuable information, advice, and guidance. The last thing you want to do is forget it!

The more calls you make, the more questions you ask, and the more information you gather, the faster you will get to the next important step in the process.

THE INTERVIEW!

Step 4: The Interview

Once you find a company that is in need of an intern and is willing to consider you, you will then be called in for an interview. This is a key moment in the process, and one to be taken VERY, VERY SERIOUSLY. They have seen your résumé. They already know your qualifications. They are calling you in to get a sense of who YOU are. How do you express yourself? Are you intelligent enough to manage their needs? Are you serious about the commitment? Will you be easygoing enough to roll with the punches of an often hectic environment? And will you represent their company positively?

This last point is a key one to consider. Will you represent them positively? Chances are they will have you go on RUNS. By this I mean go on out-of-house assignments where you will be responsible for picking up and/or delivering materials. During these runs you will be interacting with their colleagues, associates, and, most importantly, their CLIENTS—the ones who pay THEIR bills! The way you dress, speak, and manage such assignments is of paramount importance because your company's clients are not seeing you as you; they are seeing you as a representative of the company you work for.

Here are a few pointers for giving the right impression in an interview:

DRESS APPROPRIATELY: Pay or no pay, this is an interview for a job. It's never a mistake to DRESS UP. I'm not saying every guy needs a jacket and tie and every gal needs a business suit, but a clean button-down shirt or blouse never hurts. Maybe even one that's tucked in! Hollywood is a casual industry and informal attire is common in the workplace, but the liberties you might enjoy once you HAVE the job are not at all the same as when you are trying to GET the job. Dressing up for your interview will give the impression that you take the opportunity seriously. It will go a long way, trust me.

SPEAK WELL: Chances are you will be handling the phones in this internship, and there is no doubt you will be interacting with people. Your prospective employer needs to feel you have the communication skills necessary to do so. Speak confidently, with intelligence and clarity. You want to give the impression that you are smart, savvy, and worthy of selection. If you struggle with self-expression, find an acting class or study public speaking. I can't tell you how invaluable the theater training of my youth has been in enabling me to speak with strength and conviction in my adult years. A strong ability to express yourself and convey intelligence with what you say can often set you above the rest when it comes to promotion down the road.

BRING A NOTEBOOK: This is a small thing, but it can really impress your interviewer. It shows that you are focused, diligent, and on top of things. This job will most likely include detailed directions and MANY tasks, so it is important to show your interviewer right at the start that you have the organizational skills necessary to tackle whatever is thrown your way.

Furthermore, you will likely be interviewing at a number of places. It will be very useful to take notes in case you are forced to choose between a few offers. Significant factors for choosing one internship over another might include the number of shows a company has in production, the numbers of shows it has coming down the pike, its reputation for internal promotion, and the number of interns (i.e., potential competition) already working at the company.

Finally, note-taking gives you the opportunity to learn (and retain!) NAMES. Even if you don't take or get a particular internship, you should always keep the names of everyone you've met. Such a contact list makes reconnecting with the company easier in the future. Also, Hollywood is smaller than you think; there's a good chance that you will run into some of these people down the road. If you are able to approach someone, use their name and remind them of yours, you will make a huge impression, which will go a long way toward building or reinforcing a relationship. This skill is something that I still use today. Remember, this business is all about WHO YOU KNOW.

BE PREPARED: I've said it before and I'll say it again, and again, and again: Nothing makes a great impression like forethought and pre-paredness. Do your detective work. Acquaint yourself with the company's credits in advance. You should know what they are producing, have seen it, and be prepared to express why you want to be a part of making it. Glean as much about the internship as you can before you get there. Familiarize yourself with the expected duties and be ready to discuss them intelligently. Have questions prepared. I guarantee that your inter-viewer will ask you if you have any. And be sure your questions suggest that you care about the RIGHT things. Brainstorm all of the types of questions you might be asked. Practice your answers. Practice steering the interview toward the skills and strengths you might want to stress.

LISTEN: A big part of nailing an interview is keeping your ears open and giving the interviewer what he is asking for. You must feel out what HE is trying to feel out. Pay attention to what HE pays attention to. If he spends 30 minutes talking about one aspect of the job and two minutes talking about another, chances are you have a good sense of what's important to him. Focus on THAT when selling your skills. Read the interviewer's per-sonality. Some will be quick and curt. They won't have the time or patience for chitchat. You need to recognize and respect this. Quickly and efficiently tell them what you have to offer. They will appreciate this and see you as someone they can work with. Others will WANT to chitchat, to talk about the weather, sports, a recent movie, or most likely THE SHOWS THEY PRODUCE. Be prepared to indulge them. They want to know that you're personable and that they can be their gabby selves around you.

LEARN FROM YOUR MISTAKES: Nobody's perfect the first time in the room, and you won't be either. There's nothing wrong with screwing up as long as you **learn from your mistakes**. If you don't get a particular internship, chances are it's not all your fault. There are a million reasons why something doesn't work out: They gave it to the boss's son, they hired back an old intern, they ran out of money, etc. No matter what the reason, it never hurts to politely ask for a little feedback. Simply ask, "Is there anything I might be able to work on for future interviews?" They may respond or not, but it's important to ask because each interview is an opportunity to do better on the next. After an interview, refer to your notes. Try to re-create the meeting in your head and assess your performance. I'm not suggesting that you become obsessive and attempt to second-guess everything you did, but if there was something glaringly wrong with your interview performance, be honest with yourself and address the issue. The more you can learn from your mistakes at every stage of your career, the faster you will rise through the ranks and the more successful you ultimately will be.

STEP 5: BE PERSISTENT

Entertainment is a competitive field. Many people want in. When going after an internship you are not just dealing with aspiring editors, you are dealing with aspiring EVERYBODY. Stick with it. Stay focused. You will be rejected and you will lose out on jobs you were convinced you'd get. This happens to everyone. Take a deep breath, learn from the experience, keep moving, always be polite, and stay positive. It's not a sprint—it's a marathon. The sooner you learn to see things this way, the sooner you'll be showing up for the first day of the rest of your career.

STEP 6: INCONVENIENCE WITH A SMILE

Once you've taken some interviews, begun developing relationships, and gotten your name out there, answer every call that comes your way. If the number reads "Unknown" or "Private Caller," answer it anyway. You don't want to miss the call that may be your one shot. Even if you are the production company's first choice, chances are they have a second and a third. And if you don't pick up your phone, they may well move on to the next.

Also, prepare for INCONVENIENCE. I can't tell you how many jobs I have been offered at the eleventh hour. Sometimes it's the night before they want me to start, or even the day of the job! It still happens today, but when I was starting out it happened ALL THE TIME. Prepare for this. Prepare to be inconvenienced and embrace it with a smile. This eleventh-hour call is, in fact, another test. It shows how flexible you will be with the unpredictable demands of the job. Keep yourself open and available. Be ready to pounce at a moment's notice, and to pounce with grace and good spirits. This kind of attitude will go a long way toward ushering you into the industry and catapulting your career.

CHAPTER 13 REVIEW

Choose the correct answers from the lettered list.

1. One of the most important elements of success in any industry, and most certainly in entertainment, is _____.
2. The ____ ____ can be intimidating. It can be daunting, but it is a crucial step in landing any kind of internship.
3. In the entertainment industry, the _____ is the most common way in.
4. In lieu of a card, what is the premier "leave behind?"
5. When starting out, prepare to be inconvenienced and embrace it with a ____.
6. Nobody's perfect the first time in the room, and you won't be either. There's nothing wrong with screwing up as long as you____ ____ ____ _____.

    a. Learn from your mistakes
    b. Smile
    c. Contacts
    d. Cold call
    e. Résumé
    f. Internship
    g. Contacts

Answers: 1-c, 2-d, 3-f, 4-e, 5-b, 6-a

THE INTERNSHIP

So you've landed the internship. CONGRATS! Maybe it took one inter-view, maybe it took twenty, but you did it—you're in the door. The hard part is over, right?

WRONG!

Steel yourself, because things are about to get down and dirty. In Hollywood an internship is the professional equivalent of pledging a fra-ternity. You do everything that everybody else doesn't want to bother with. It's often less than glamorous and generally menial. The key, though, is to recognize that this is a test. You are being observed. Your new bosses are assessing how you handle the unimportant assignments, determining whether to give you MORE IMPORTANT ones. Also, they are assessing whether or not you are someone they enjoy working with. They are look-ing at your attitude, especially in moments of stress, so keep that smile on your face, that skip in your step, and your eye on the prize.

Getting in is one thing; staying in and moving up, that's THE thing! And here's how it's done.

STEP 1: THE TRIAL PERIOD

Most new jobs start with a TRIAL PERIOD. And the internship is no different. An intern's trial period usually lasts about a month. Your only concern during this time should be *your job and nothing but your job*. You need to take it seriously, do it well, and have a smile on your face while you're at it. Be friendly, easygoing, always willing, but never intrusive. Embrace each assignment with enthusiasm and keep your fatigue and stress to yourself.

As an intern I quickly mastered the art of staying in people's good graces. My trick? I took every single assignment, even the most trivial, as seriously as I might the fate of my entire career. One of my first internships was working for the late director Alan J. Pakula on his film *The Devil's Own*, starring Harrison Ford and Brad Pitt. One of my main responsibilities was grocery shopping. And, no, not grocery shopping for Ford and Pitt, nothing nearly as glamorous. Instead, I was grocery shopping for the director's personal office—an office that sat mostly vacant, as everyone who mattered was on the set making a movie. So I was basically shopping for no one. Even so, there was a list of very specific items that needed to be in that kitchen just in case someone of import showed up and wanted to nosh. And driven to impress, I obsessed over every single one of them. I wouldn't just buy chips, I would purchase the exact brand, flavor, and serving size requested. If one store didn't have the right sugar-free, all-natural fruit sodas, I was off to another. And I had already done the research to know where the other local stores were, how much extra time my visits to them would cost me, and how to adjust my other assignments to stay on schedule. Overkill perhaps, but that kind of over-preparation and attention to detail was great training for the kind of diligence and forethought necessary to survive the rigors of Hollywood. In fact, it was within these assignments that I honed the work ethic and attitude that have dictated the trajectory of my entire career. My diligence also VERY quickly got me past my trial period and into the good graces of my superiors. I made great contacts, stayed on that internship for almost a year, and count it as one of the most valuable learning experiences of my career.

STEP 2: MAKE FRIENDS

"Half the job is getting along with other people."

Jackson Anderer, Editor,
Extreme Makeover: Home Edition and *Celebrity Apprentice*

At some point, probably around your first-month anniversary, your trial period will end. You'll know it when it happens because there will be more familiarity and trust offered you by your boss. You'll start enjoying earnest compliments on the quality of your work. Others around you will become more comfortable saying hello and chatting with you. They will know that you're no longer on the potential chopping block and will relax around you.

Once you've gotten to this point, it's time to start building relationships. As I've said, this business is all about WHO YOU KNOW. The majority of all hires in the entertainment industry come through personal referrals. And since your goal is for this internship to lead to a job, it's time to starting getting to know all those people who can refer you!

I like to enter into every new workplace treating everyone as if they are ALREADY my friend. My philosophy is, "You are my friend until you prove otherwise. I will respect you until you give me reason not to." Be yourself. Be friendly. Leave judgments at the door. Join in conversations and build on shared interests. And always, always, always accept social invitations. This is how you truly build those personal connections. After-hours and free from the pressures of the workplace, people are much more apt to let their hair down and much more willing to let YOU in.

Some of the most important friendships you will forge in the workplace are with your most immediate collaborators—the other interns. There is no one better with whom to commiserate and no one more important to encourage and support. Special bonds often form among peers who come up together. There's a loyalty and compassion for one another that is rare and can prove enduring. Remember, these peers are climbing the same ladders that you're climbing, and as they rise they will be in positions to recommend others—including YOU. Nurture these relationships and maintain them. Support others as you would have them support you. Some of my closest friends and business relationships to this day are the women and men I came up with. I would not be NEAR where I am without them.

STEP 3: SELF-PROMOTE

Once you've begun building new friendships and revealing more of yourself and your personality, it is time to start SELF PROMOTING. It is time to discuss your immediate goals and share your long-term aspirations. In short, it's time to talk POST!

Your goal right now is to work toward landing a paying job, and as an aspiring reality TV editor, the job you're shooting for is that of a POST-PRODUCTION ASSISTANT (Post PA). Most of the time the best way to land this position is through internal promotion and/or direct referral, so start laying that groundwork. Start spreading word of your ambitions around the office. Ask if there's a chance you might be able to tour the company's postproduction facilities and perhaps introduce yourself to the *Post Coordinator* and *Post Supervisor*, both of whom deal with hiring Post PAs.

The timing for these requests is critical. You don't want to demand too much too soon, and always, always, always remember that the quality of your work as an intern comes first. Nobody's going to want to promote or refer you if you're doing a crappy job! But ALSO remember that you are giving them free labor. It's your right to ask for this kind of exposure in return.

Take Note: Beware the Dead Ends

There are some internships that WON'T help you get to where you're headed. These are often referred to as DEAD ENDS, and it is important to spot them quickly.

Once you are beyond your trial period, start to read your surroundings. Study the lay of the land. Observe the people who will decide your fate. Try to gauge their opinion of you and their proclivity for nurturing others. Assess their penchant for promoting. There may be any number of reasons why someone might not want to help you move up: personality conflict, competition, jealousy, finances, conceit, forgetfulness...too many to list. But if you see that things are not moving forward; if people are not connecting with you and reassuring you that they are happy with your work; if people are not interested in learning more about your aspirations; if other interns and employees complain about lack of promotion across the board; or if you are refused or disregarded when you ask for opportunities to explore their post facilities and meet their post-people—jump ship!

It can take months of free labor to get to the next level. The last thing you want to do is waste those months on a DEAD END. So if you happen into the wrong environment, recognize it quickly, step away, regroup, and try again.

STEP 4: STEP UP

Okay, so your internship has progressed positively. You've kept the level and quality of your work high. You've cultivated relationships. You've carefully spread the word that postproduction is where you want to be and you have taken advantage of every opportunity to expose yourself to that department and the people who manage it. If all of this is true, then at a certain point the question of employment will come up. If not by your employers, then certainly you should do it for them.

Traditionally, an unspoken understanding exists between an employer and an intern: You are there to learn and to prove yourself capable. If satisfied, your employer should help you STEP UP to the next level. Guiding you toward an actual paying job is your employer's duty. That's the deal. It might be through direct internal promotion or referral to an outside company, but after a dedicated, hardworking stint as an intern, it is your right as a reliable and respected employee to expect a boost. Again, you need to pace yourself. You can't ask for too much too soon. Still, if you live up to your half of the bargain, your employers need to live up to theirs.

As I said, the job you will be targeting next is that of the POST-PRODUCTION ASSISTANT. It is the natural next step for any intern looking to get into post. And it is the first official rung on the editorial ladder.

CHAPTER 14 REVIEW

Choose the correct answers from the lettered list.

1. As an intern, your goal is to work toward landing a paying job, and as an aspiring reality TV editor, the initial job you're shooting for is that of a _____ _____.

2. The majority of all hires in the entertainment industry come through

    _____ _____.

3. There are some internships that WON'T help you get to where you're headed. These are referred to as ____ ____, and it is important to spot them quickly.

4. Most new jobs start with a _____ _____. It usually lasts about a month. Your only concern during this time should be *your job and nothing but your job.*

    a. Dead ends
    b. Trial period
    c. Personal referrals
    d. Postproduction assistant

Answers: 1-d, 2-c, 3-a, 4-b

CHAPTER 15

THE POST PA

The job of a production assistant (PA) is more or less a paid version of an internship. You are still required to do the less important and less flattering tasks—and to like them. You are still in the process of proving yourself. You must still maintain a high quality of work and work ethic, despite the fact that you may not be working your dream job. The only difference is now you are actually on the payroll, and that is a HUGE difference. An intern is seen as a practice employee. They aren't taken all that seriously, and they are given latitude when it comes to screw-ups and missteps. As a PA things are a little different. If you screw up too much, you get fired, not forgiven.

As a POSTPRODUCTION ASSISTANT, or POST PA, you are an assistant assigned exclusively to the post department. Your job is to make runs (pickups and deliveries), take lunch orders, and manage the clerical duties necessary to maintain the editorial department. You are the runner, the gofer, and the runt of the editorial team. BUT you are still a part of the editorial team, and that makes all the difference. Now you have access to the entire process. You can observe, ask carefully timed questions, and start to build practical hands-on skills. Most importantly, you can start to build relationships with the people who will directly determine your climb to the editor's chair.

STEP 1: ALWAYS BE READY FOR EVERYTHING

"A good PA is a mind reader. They are always anticipating. They know what needs to be done before they are asked. The less direction they need, the more quickly they will get promoted."

Cindy Scott, Post Supervisor

As a post PA your assignments may seem menial. They may appear trivial, but looks can be deceiving. However pedestrian the post PA job may feel, it is absolutely *essential* work. And no postproduction department can survive without it. Whenever an unwelcome surprise occurs—the Internet is down, something breaks, a deadline is missed, someone quits, NBC needs that cut *immediately*—the post PA must jump into action. The post PA needs to be on call at all times, ready to roll at a moment's notice. The editors are under the gun with no time for meal breaks: Grab some petty cash and start taking lunch orders. The tapes have returned from the field completely mislabeled and out of order: Grab a pen, press PLAY and start making sense of the madness.

A great post PA regularly checks in and checks up on everyone in the department. Post PAs absorb every aspect of the postproduction machine, oiling it as they go about their duties. They learn the particulars of each and every one of their superiors, and they cater to them. A great post PA spots a problem or potential problem before others notice it and handles it before anyone can utter a word.

Adopting this approach will help you cruise through the ever important trial period (remember, there's one for every new job) and into the good graces of your colleagues. And it is from these good graces that will spring *opportunity*.

STEP 2: LET'S GET TECHNICAL

> *"I would take copious notes and organize them into a Word document nightly. That way I could always go back and reference everything. You need to ask questions, you just don't want to keep asking them twice."*
>
> George Dybas, Editor,
> *Police Women of Dallas* and *Restaurant Stakeout*

Once you have mastered the art of always being ready for everything, once you have proven yourself and your position is secure, it is now time to start capitalizing on your proximity to your goal job. It's time to start juicing the "post" part of your title for all it's worth. BUT before you can swing for the creative fences of actual editing, you first must pay your TECHNICAL dues. So, it's time to get technical!

In order for an editor to work competently and get the job done efficiently, all OTHER aspects of the postproduction process must run smoothly. The actual cutting of picture and sound are just a part of bringing a show from the field to the screen: The raw footage and all related elements (sound effects, music, miscellaneous audio, etc.) must be ingested, manipulated, and organized. Cuts must be exported, posted, copied, and burned. Sound must be mixed, consolidated, transferred, and laid back. Picture must be upressed (have its resolution upped, i.e., be uncompressed), color corrected, output, and delivered, and that doesn't even begin to touch upon the constant maintenance and eleventh-hour troubleshooting required to keep such a massive, networked computing system on its feet.

Your head is probably spinning right now. Don't worry, when I started out, mine was too. I was about as "technical" and "computer savvy" as an eighty-year-old grandmother, but slowly, surely, I picked up the knowledge. I learned the ropes. And as a post PA you are in the perfect position to do the exact same thing. But to accomplish this, to begin absorbing the process and the skills, you must first memorize two very important words—**ASSISTANT EDITOR**. (Burn them into your brain and repeat them again and again to yourself. These two words should be your post PA mantra.)

The ASSISTANT EDITOR (AE) is the editor's right hand. AEs are the overseers of all that is technical. They are the go-to jacks-of-all-post-production-trade. All that stuff I rattled off above? THEY do that! And they are the ones you must listen to and learn from. They are your mentors and role models, *so start observing*. Ask carefully timed questions and have a notebook handy to record the answers. Present yourself as an interested, eager, responsible apprentice. And *always* be willing to offer up your free time whenever they might need it.

Why? Because it is the AE position that you aspire to next!

STEP 3: WHAT FREE TIME?

As a post PA on Universal Pictures' *The Rocky and Bullwinkle Movie*, I was determined to learn, and I made sure the right people knew it. When the clock struck quitting time and others ran for the door, I stayed behind. Even if there was nothing to do, I stayed behind—JUST TO STAY BEHIND. I made it known that I was eager to learn and happy to take on any job that needed doing. Gradually, my after-hours presence became noticed. My identity started to shift. I was no longer just another post PA—I was "Jeff, the hardworking, ambitious up-and-comer who is obviously serious about his career and serious about learning."

Most employers won't be interested in having you learn the job of an assistant editor while being paid to do the job of a post PA. You are being given cash money in exchange for very specific services. If you want to do more, if you want to expand your knowledge and skills, you're going to have to sacrifice your late nights, your early mornings, and potentially even your weekends. That said, if you're eager, willing to sacrifice and continue to cultivate highly important relationships, it's not THAT hard to get a few after-hours lessons. (Especially if the assistant editors giving the lessons know that once you learn the ropes YOU can start doing THEIR work for them!)

That's the deal. The AE gives you the skills, then you repay him by helping to shoulder his burden free of charge. This may sound unfair, but it really isn't. The moment you start learning the AE's technical skills and successfully implementing them in the workplace, you cease to be a just another post PA. Suddenly you transform into something much more valuable—an AE in training!

The more time you offer up to learning the AE's job and the more practice you have at it, the more valuable you will become. The new skills you acquire and the new identity you quickly establish with your superiors will put you first in line for promotion—and that's exactly where you want to be.

STEP 4: KNOW YOUR SH!T

So what ARE these skills that you need to start learning? What IS this technical know-how that every AE must acquire? Well, there are a few ESSENTIALS, and as your kind and generous professor, I have listed them below to give you a leg up on the competition. At first glance, it might seem logical to list the skills of an AE in the upcoming chapter on BEING an AE, but the truth is you won't GET the AE job unless you know how do it first. So here you go!

INGESTING THE MEDIA: In order to manipulate the footage in an edit, you first must HAVE footage to manipulate. Ingesting the media is the process of transferring footage from the camera it was shot on to the computer you will be working on. This is an assistant editor's most time-consuming job. It is also the easiest, AND the easiest for an AE to walk away from if you, the post PA, prove that you've got it handled.

There are two basic ways to ingest the media. The first is by *digitizing* tapes—which quite literally means connecting a tape deck to your computer and playing the taped footage as the computer records it digitally onto a hard drive. The second way to ingest is by *importing* or *transferring* the footage. More and more frequently these days, video is being shot and edited using what is called a *tapeless workflow*. This simply means that instead of putting a TAPE in a camera and pressing RECORD you are now slipping a DRIVE or MEDIA CARD into a camera and pressing CAPTURE. Since the tapeless footage is captured directly to a drive, there is no need for a tape deck. You merely *copy* or *move* media files from the camera's hard drive to the computer's hard drive. It is the same principle as moving a song from your computer to your iPod or moving a photo from a flash card to your computer. (Note: The specifics of moving media differ from one non-linear editing system to another, but the basic concept is universal.)

Ingesting media is a fairly simple procedure, BUT it still requires your full attention, especially when you are first starting out. Take copious notes whenever you receive instruction, and review them again and again as you go. All too often the easiest tasks will get the least amount of attention, and this is where BIG mistakes can be made. I can't tell you how many times, when I was starting out, I would lose my focus, miss some important setting, and have to re-digitize hours of footage. The LAST thing you want to do is to make a mistake while covering for an AE who is giving you a shot in his or her seat. That could cost you a promotion.

ORGANIZING THE EDIT: The second and probably most far-reaching technical skill you need to acquire is that of **editorial organization**. A strong system of organization in post is essential to the success of any show, and it is the AE's job to design and maintain this system. Footage must be broken down into small clips, which are then labeled and arranged to give the editor clear and easy access to them. SFX and music must be separated by type and arranged by genre. Various versions of various cuts must be slated (labeled with pertinent information: title, version number, running time, etc.), dated, and backed up.

It is imperative that at any point, anything that anyone needs—any and every picture clip and piece of audio—can be easily located and accessed. A good AE remains on top of this work at all times. Every piece of the yet-to-be-assembled puzzle, no matter how small, must have a clear and discernible home from which it can be retrieved with only a moment's notice. Once you have your hands on an Avid manual, some important terms to familiarize yourself with are: *sub-clipping, stacking, grouping, multi-group, multi-cam, bin display, clip coloring, binning*, and *labeling*.

OUTPUTTING AND EXPORTING: Often, there are network executives and producers who never make it to the edit bay. Sometimes they are out of town or even out of the country. However, they still require inclusion in the editing process. They want to see the show's cuts as they progress and offer their two cents' worth in shaping the finished product. So, at various points in the process, edited sequences must be converted into a form that is transportable/transmittable and viewable OUT-OF-HOUSE. The two basic ways to do this are via **Outputting** and **Exporting**.

Outputting (a technique that is becoming less and less common these days) is the process of feeding a sequence out of the computer onto a physical videotape or DVD. *Exporting* is the process of converting a sequence into a digital audio-video file that can then be transmitted via the Internet. It is the AE's responsibility to oversee these processes. Attention to detail is crucial: It must be the right version (generally the editor's most current) of the right cut or sequence that is output or converted. It must sound right, look good, and it must be labeled clearly and accurately. Sending a network executive the wrong version of the wrong cut is a mistake that can get even the best AE booted from a gig!

EXPORTING AUDIO: Once the cutting is complete and picture has been LOCKED (declared to be in its final edited state), the edit moves into its FINISHING PHASE. Typically, the audio portion of said cut will be finalized or "sweetened" (extraneous noises removed, appropriate reverbs added, etc.) out-of-house. To facilitate this, the audio elements must be **exported** from the computer and converted into what are called AAF (advanced authoring format) files, which are compatible with the sound-design programs used in most out-of-house audio facilities.

(NOTE: As a part of the process of sending your audio out-of-house, it is common to send a QuickTime video of your edit also, so that your sound designer has a visual reference to consult.)

UPRESSING/ONLINING: Often, when first ingested into the computer, footage will be compressed to conserve space. The specifics of digital compression are a bit technical, but all you really need to understand is that the ingested video will take up less computer hard drive space and look fuzzier when it is compressed. It will look quite similar to the fuzzy videos you might see on YouTube. These too are compressed.

It will remain at this lower quality throughout the editing process, but once picture has locked and the show moves into its finishing phase, high quality must be restored. To do this, the picture must be re-ingested, this time at the highest resolution possible. This process is referred to as **upressing** or **onlining** the cut. Essentially, you are replacing the fuzzy images with clear ones. Once you have your hands on an Avid manual, some important terms to familiarize yourself with are: *offline media*, *decomposing*, *re-linking*, *batch importing*, and *rendering*.

MEDIA MANAGEMENT: This is the most involved of all the AE's responsibilities. All media that is ingested is usually stored on one massive, expandable multi–hard drive unit, the most popular of which is called the Avid Unity ISIS, or simply ISIS for short. The ISIS is a huge stack of dozens of interconnected drives that work together as one big mega-drive that allows simultaneous access to the same media from more than one workstation. If a show has a few editors working simultaneously, all of their editing stations connect to ISIS, from which each editor can draw media at any time.

The assistant editor must carefully MAINTAIN the ISIS system, and carefully manage the media within it. The AE must watch where and how his project's media is saved, ensuring that no individual drive (or "workspace" as it is technically termed) becomes too full. Often the assistant must move media from drive to drive to make room for incoming new projects. The AE might also have to delete and backup media and other project info as shows are completed and go into storage.

I know this technical stuff sounds like brain surgery at this point, but trust me, it isn't. It's just like driving: Once you get behind the wheel it quickly becomes second nature. BUT, also just as with driving, it requires careful attention and focus to keep things moving smoothly. The last thing you want to do is screw up the mother ship of the media or fry the brain center of the system. Those kinds of mistakes aren't easy to cover up. That is the kind of thing that can bring the entire post process to a grinding halt.

TROUBLESHOOTING: Whenever there is a computer crash, a freeze, a monitor glitch, or just about any other technical problem, it is the assistant editor's responsibility to solve it. There is no science to learning this stuff. Mostly, it's trial by fire. You do have help, though. Many production companies rent their computer editing systems, and associated with the rental is a tech support line ready to talk you through even the worst technical hiccups. In the beginning of your stint as an AE you will call that number A LOT. (I know I did.) You will also depend on the experience of assistant editors who have been there longer than you. But slowly, over time, you will begin to get a handle on most of the common technical problems and memorize their various solutions.

And So...

There you have it. The basics of assistant editing all jammed into the post PA chapter. Learn as much of this stuff as early as you can. If you do, you'll be bumped up to the next level in no time, and you'll have some new post PA doing YOUR work for YOU!

Chapter 15 Review

Choose the correct answers from the lettered list.

1. The _____ _____ is the editor's right hand. He or she oversees all that is technical and is the go-to jack-of-all-postproduction-trades.

2. As a post PA trying to learn the job of the assistant editor, you must always be willing to give up what in order to get ahead?

3. The most far-reaching technical skill every assistant editor needs to acquire is that of _____ _____.

4. What do you call the process of transferring footage from the camera it was shot on to the computer you will be working on?

5. A great post PA must _____ __ _____ ___ _____.

6. When climbing the postproduction ladder, before you can swing for the creative fences of actual editing, you first must pay your _____ dues.

    a. Always be ready for everything
    b. Assistant editor
    c. Editorial organization
    d. Your free time
    e. Ingesting the media
    f. Technical

Answers: 1-b, 2-d, 3-c, 4-e, 5-a, 6-f

CHAPTER 16

THE AE

Welcome to the intense rite of passage we call ASSISTANT EDITING. You may not be a full-fledged editor, but you DO have "editor" in your title and that is a huge deal. Your first assignment: *Reread the last chapter.* Get an Avid Users manual. Get that at-home editing system. Master the technical aspects of the job.

As an assistant editor, your job is to support the editor and the editorial process from start to finish. You bring the footage in. You organize and distribute it. You maintain technical control over it. You support creative fluidity. And you oversee the completion and ultimate delivery of the final product. But, as your job title might suggest, you are also an EDITOR-IN-TRAINING. You are a ladder rung away from your end goal. and now, more than ever, it is time to prove you have what it takes to step up and take the reins.

Strictly speaking, your job is not to edit. BUT, at the same time, you will never be promoted to editor if you DON'T edit. Don't you love Catch-22s? Hollywood sure does. So, just as with your internship and just as with your post PA gig, say goodbye to your after-work hours, and say hello to free labor!

STEP 1: EDIT

"Ask for small projects to cut on your own time (teases, short segments, cold opens, etc.)...then do a great job and turn it around quickly. It's a perfect chance to showcase your skills, prove that you respect deadlines, and [demonstrate that you] are someone that can be relied upon."

Sabrina Mar, Producer,
Catfish: The TV Show and *Extreme Makeover: Home Edition*

With the job of assistant editor, as with every position you will hold before it, there is a trial period. So, do your job well. Work hard. Be as *organized* as possible. And, most importantly, be positive and eager to please. No one will give you more work if they are not confident that you can handle what you already have. (I know, I know, broken record. But these things cannot be stressed enough!)

Once your trial period is over, and you know that your employers are comfortable with you and confident in your abilities—once you know that your AE job is safe—it is time to start nurturing your relationships with the editors themselves. Let it be known that you want to edit and you are willing to assist their cuts in any way you can. Do they need *stringouts* (an assembly of a scene's most promising selects) put together at night? Do they want you to do a SFX pass (enhancing a scene by fitting in choice SFX)? Do they need their rough cut mixed before it is screened? Do they need minor sequences, montages, or teases put together but have no time to do it themselves? The more work the editors give you—and the more of this work that you accomplish on time and well executed—the more they will trust you and start thinking of you, not as an ASSISTANT but as an EDITOR and a peer. This is the key to every promotion: Your superiors, those who have the power to get you your next job, need to see you in that job already. Train them to see you as you see yourself—as an Editor.

"As an editor I love finding AEs that WANT to edit. Honestly, it's a breath of fresh air. It's amazing how many assists never approach me, never ask to cut anything, never even ask for tips on how to move up. Honestly it blows me away. When I was an assist, all I wanted to do was edit. Who wouldn't?"

Tim Roche, Editor,
It's Always Sunny in Philadelphia and *Undercover Boss*

STEP 2: DELIVER

I remember my first big opportunity very clearly. I was an assistant editor on the Fox reality show *Anything for Love*, and I had been expressing my interest in cutting for some time. Finally, one evening my post supervisor came to me and said there was a scene that the executive producer was unhappy with. It just wasn't coming together. To make matters worse, it needed to be done ASAP and none of the show's editors could spare the time to fix it. He challenged me to give it a go. Despite the fact that it was the end of rather long day and I was just packing to leave, I eagerly accepted. The timing was less than ideal BUT THAT DIDN'T MATTER. This was the shot I had been waiting for and I wasn't going to screw it up.

That night was one of the longest I can remember. I worked my ass off. I cut and recut and recut. I needed to come up with a fresh approach that would impress the boss, but I also needed to be true to the style that had already been established for the show. I needed to use strong interviews and nail the music. I wanted it to be perfect because I knew that a good job could mean a promotion. And I knew that a crappy job could mean NO MORE SHOTS! I finished my cut just as the sun came up, ran home, caught a few hours of sleep, and then quickly returned for a fresh day of work. (NOTE: I'm not advocating sleepy driving. Push yourself, but not at the risk of health and safety.)

It paid off. The executive producer loved it. He was impressed, and he immediately began seeing me in a new light. More after-hours assignments quickly followed, and I treated each one with the same intense focus and dedication. I kept delivering the goods, and within a month I got my promotion. I was officially an editor! I doubled my pay, tripled my respect, and never looked back.

Getting the opportunity to cut is one thing, but doing the job right is THE thing. When you are given "off the clock" editing opportunities, TAKE THEM SERIOUSLY. Do your absolute best. You want these first assignments to instill confidence in your superiors. You want to change your identity in their eyes. This is your chance to impress. This is the reason you've been practice-editing at home. This is the reason you bought and read this book!

Quick Tip: Soliciting Feedback

It never hurts to get a little editorial feedback before unveiling your work to the boss. This is especially true when you are just starting out. Choose an editor or a producer whom you trust and whom you know your boss respects. Solicit this colleague's guidance with discretion. They've been through it. Often their small tips and suggestions will help you deliver exactly what your boss wants to see.

STEP 3: ADVERTISE

> *"When trying to move up to a full-time editor position, don't be afraid to sell yourself and remind people again and again of what you want. It may feel a little pushy, but the truth is that sometimes a little push is a good thing."*
>
> Sax Eno, Editor,
> *Hell's Kitchen* and *The Real World*

As your superiors' trust in you begins to develop and as you continue to turn in more and more successful after-hours assignments, spread the word. Don't wait around for your promotion to come to you; go to it. Chase after it. Post supervisors, post co-coordinators, executive producers, and anyone else who might move you up the ladder are busy people. They have a lot on their plates, and it's easy for them to forget the eager young assistant slaving long into the night to get ahead. You need to make it your mission to politely *remind* them that you would love the opportunity to work as an editor if the position presented itself. Tell them that if they need someone to work at night or if they have a weekend emergency, you are their guy. Let them know you are on call 24/7 to step up and do the job.

I promise, the more dedicated and focused you are with this gentle but persistent self-promotion, while continuing to deliver the goods they require, the faster your promotion will come. Obviously you don't want to be *too* pushy. As with anything else, including editing itself, timing is everything. Still, if you are delivering the goods, you deserve to reap the benefit.

STEP 4: ONCE AGAIN, ALWAYS BEWARE OF DEAD ENDS

Unfortunately, the higher you climb the more conscious you must be of your superiors' inclinations or lack of inclinations for promoting from within their ranks. Each step up comes with a new and much greater level of responsibility. As such, some supervisors will be a bit gun-shy about promoting AEs to the editor position. They feel it's too much of a risk. The job of an editor is critical, and choosing the wrong person for the chair can cause a show major setbacks. They're afraid that if things go wrong, they will be held accountable for hiring someone ill-prepared for the job.

Many times a post supervisor will decide to hire a complete stranger with a fancy-looking résumé over the proven, competent, hardworking AE standing right in front of him. In my opinion, this attitude is based in small-minded, fear-based ignorance. Yet I've seen it time and again. And often these "strangers" turn out to be complete duds. They end up costing the company and the show thousands of dollars in wasted time and useless work, and yet some post supervisors cannot see the forest for the trees. They just don't get that you—the motivated AE—will work ten times as hard as the imported stranger to prove yourself and do the job right. (Not to mention that you actually KNOW the show already and have had heaps of practice at putting it together during your free after-hours assignments.) As frustrating as this can be, it happens. So keep an eye out for the superior with a fear-based aversion to internal promotion, and jump ship when you see it.

Another obstacle in your ascension can be a supervisor who doesn't want to lose you and your skills as an AE. Although he or she may know that you can do the job of an editor, this supervisor may still decide not to promote you because he or she doesn't want to sacrifice what you're already giving the show! Finding a good AE is not so easy. It requires a very specific knowledge base, attention to detail, and a strong work ethic. Sometimes this is more than a supervisor is willing to give up. If you think that might be the case with your supervisor—get out!

I know it may be painful to abandon a company that you have put time and effort into, but it's better to sacrifice your past time and effort than to waste your future on a pointless pursuit. Find an "assist" job somewhere else, and continue your climb with the same approach.

STEP 5: ACCEPT IT WITH A SMILE

Like every other opportunity in your climb to the editor's job, the bump up to editor could very likely come at the eleventh hour and entirely unexpectedly. It may offer less money than anticipated and much less desirable hours than you currently enjoy (my first editing shift was graveyard). Still, no matter how it comes, and how less-than-ideal its demands may be, you need to be ready to accept it with a smile.

- "I know it's Sunday night, but can you start TONIGHT?"
- "Do you think you could do a double shift of assisting *and* editing for a while?"
- "I can't really pay you the editor rate, but I can give you the work."
- "How does *right now* sound? And we need it finished in an hour!"

Nothing worth doing comes easy, and dues must be paid. Always stay eager and be prepared to work your ass off. Getting the gig is one thing; KEEPING the gig is something else entirely.

Take Note: Another Way

The traditional career path for an aspiring editor involves a period of tenure as an assistant editor. But in recent years, another path to that job goal has emerged. With growing frequency, STORY PRODUCERS are being outfitted with their very own editing stations so that they can search footage and prepare stringouts for the editor. This affords them a unique opportunity. They learn to use an editing program, and if they're so inclined, they can also practice and hone editing skills. These skills coupled with their already developed storytelling chops make them viable candidates for promotion to editor. In truth, both paths can lead to the same end as long as your approach is correct. If you are willing to give up your free time, take on after-hours editorial assignments, and do the job right, you'll find yourself a full-fledged editor in no time.

CHAPTER 16 REVIEW

Choose the correct answers from the lettered list.

1. As your superiors' trust in you begins to develop, and as you continue to turn in more and more successful after-hours assignments, take it upon yourself to do what?

2. Getting the opportunity to cut is one thing, but what is THE thing?

3. Always keep an eye out for the dead ends, know how to spot them, and ____ ____ if you do.

4. No matter how your first promotion comes, and how less-than-ideal its demands may be, you always need to be ready to _____ __ ____ _ ____.

5. It never hurts to get a little _____ _____ before unveiling your work to the boss.

   a. Jump ship
   b. Spread the word
   c. Doing the job right
   d. Accept it with a smile
   e. Editorial feedback

Answers: 1-b, 2-c, 3-a, 4-d, 5-e

CHAPTER 17

THE EDITOR...OR, KEEPING THE GIG!

"Think about how many decisions you make in a day. Multiply that by 1,000 and you have a day in reality editing. That's our job description."

Anthony Rivard, Editor,
Top Chef and *The X Factor*

So you've done it. You are now an official reality TV editor. You worked hard, you kept focused, you followed the steps and you have reaped your reward. (And right now you are busy writing me an enthusiastic thank-you letter.) But hold on, not so fast. You're not finished yet. You may HAVE the job, but now you have a new challenge before you. Now, you need to KEEP it.

The position of editor is among the most important in reality TV. It is one of the field's highest-paid gigs, and quite possibly THE most creatively responsible one. For these reasons it is also one of the most at-risk jobs. The sad fact is that when a show is in trouble, the editor is all too often the scapegoat. This is especially true if you are recently promoted and thus new to the job. This doesn't necessarily mean that a show's problems are your fault; it just means that editors are easy fodder. They are easy to point a finger at and tear down when a production company or a producer needs to save face.

So how do you protect yourself? How do you guard against the Hollywood blame game? How do you avoid getting axed, especially when you are the freshest recruit in the editorial department? Well, I've NEVER been fired, never even come close to being fired—and here's what I've done to keep it that way.

1. GET TO KNOW THE SHOW

Often you will be hired onto a show already in progress. It might be three weeks, three months, or even three seasons old! That said, if you are lucky enough to come in midstream, the very first things you want to do are study and mimic the EARLIER EPISODES.

Ask around. Get a sense of which editor(s) your superiors like and which cuts they have been impressed by. Study those cuts carefully, taking detailed notes. Pay attention to the many editorial techniques and decisions we discussed earlier in this book. How were bites used? What KINDS of bites did they favor? How was music used? Was it WALL-TO-WALL or sparse? Is VO used? If so, how does it drive the scene? How montage-heavy is the show? How about graphics and SFX? By choosing the right editor and the right cuts to study and emulate, you can not only absorb that editor's choices, you can also learn about the style and substance of his or her BOSS'S CHOICES. (And that boss is YOUR BOSS too!) And the sooner you can start delivering *cuts tailored to meet your BOSS's tastes*, the more secure your position will be.

Sometimes I will actually copy a favored editor's music choices into a new bin. Then, if I have a similar scene or dramatic moment, I will try to find like-sounding cues by referencing this bin and listening to what has already been used successfully. I will do the same with graphics, SFX, and even title fonts. I'm sure you've heard the saying *"Good artists borrow, great artists steal."* Well, in reality TV, *"Good editors reference, smart editors duplicate, sample, copy, paste, and just about everything else they can think of."* So, after you are doubly sure that your superiors LIKED the choices you're about to steal—then copy, copy, copy!

This practice has saved me again and again at the start of a new job. As soon as your employer sees and feels the show they are trying to make *embodied in your work*, you will not only have job security, you will quickly become coveted and championed as one of the few who actually "GET IT."

2. ASK QUESTIONS

When you step into a new job, especially if you've just been promoted, you must quickly take in a LOT of new information. Any new position requires a period of orientation. Multiply the average job's orientation difficulty by fifty and you have reality TV editing's orientation curve. With this in mind, there is one golden rule to remember: *Never be afraid to ask questions.* Use discretion, of course, and be careful about what, whom, and when you ask. You don't want to appear incompetent, but still, don't be afraid to ask. In the end it's better to ask and do it right than to make the wrong decisions and end up with a bad cut.

The first people I usually consult are the editors who are turning out the most popular edits. If it's too soon to determine which guys and gals are turning out the popular cuts, just figure out who the veterans at the company are, and who has been hired again and again by your boss. They are the ones most likely to know and "GET" the boss's style. Often, when I'm just settling in, I will have these editors pre-screen my first few cuts and give me pointers. Seasoned editors are priceless sources of guidance and support, and generally they are happy to help. They've been you; they know what it's like. And if they are lead editors, they very likely will be inheriting your work to polish for airing. Trust me, I would much rather help a new editor do the job right the first time, so that I don't have to overhaul it down the line.

After editors, I would next bring my queries to my immediate superiors and/or collaborators—the story producers. They are there to assist and guide you. Use them. When story or style questions arise, go to them, get them involved. (FYI: They are also a great resource in determining which cuts to study and editors to mimic.) Story producers are there to serve as the eyes and ears of the executive producer—your boss. Their job is to focus your edit and usher it to a reasonable shape for receiving critical notes and final polish. Heed their advice.

3. BEWARE! NOT ALL PRODUCERS ARE CREATED EQUAL

Here is one important piece of story producer advice: *Not all story producers are created equal.* So, you need to carefully assess YOUR story producer right from the get-go. To be fair, the majority of producers I have worked with over the years have been great. Their sharp instincts and years of experience have only made me a stronger, more sensitive storyteller. But every now and then you'll draw the short straw and be assigned a producer whose misguided direction will unwittingly undermine your work, and when it comes time to screen it for your boss, you will be the one taking the fall.

There are generally two ways to assess the value of a story producer. The first and quickest is to once again ASK THE EDITORS. Chances are they've worked with this person before and have well-considered opinions about him or her. I wouldn't necessarily ask flat-out who sucks and who rocks. (Use a little tact, please.) Rather, casually and subtly feel out your fellow editors' opinions, and then use their perspectives to guide your decisions moving forward.

The second way to assess the strength of your producer is through your own careful and focused observation of them. If he or she is working with other editors, follow the process and take note of the outcome. Did the eventual screening with the boss go well? If not, how much of that was because of the producer? Also, feel out the progression of your own collaboration. How do you feel about the producer's suggestions? Does he "get it"? And how are your screenings playing out based on his direction? One bad screening is all I've ever needed to come to a very quick and absolute opinion on the value of my collaborator and his notes.

In the event that you *do* draw that dreaded short straw and your producer *is* less than competent, you still must handle the situation delicately. Initially, if not throughout the process, you *do* need to follow at least *some* of that person's direction. Technically you are required to do what he or she says—at least some of the time. That's your job. But you should try your best to hedge your bets. Perhaps offer alternatives to bad suggestions. Perhaps use time as an excuse to address only the least undermining notes. If all else fails and your job is truly on the line, I would ask the most senior editor for advice. Usually a lead editor has a bit of pull. Often he or she can sidestep the many story producers and address the executive producer directly if the situation demands it. If you can get this person on your side, he or she will at least have your back if any question of your competency arises.

Whenever you are forced to work with an incompetent, the politics of the situation can be very tricky. The only consolation I can offer is that if your collaborators really are that weak, chances are they won't be around for long, and more than likely when they do go, they will be replaced by someone great.

Take Note: Know Your Hierarchy

Make sure you learn the hierarchy of the producing staff. When determining when and how to sidestep a producer's notes, it is important to know exactly what type of producer he or she is. Know the difference between the associate producers, the story producers, the senior producers, the supervising producers, the co-executive producers, and the executive producers. When dealing with a story producer you can get a bit creative with how and when you address that person's notes. When you are dealing with a supervising producer or above, you absolutely CANNOT get creative! This is someone who really is in charge. He or she has the power to fire you on the spot. Whether you agree or disagree, you MUST do exactly what a supervising producer says—and do it with a smile every time.

THE PRODUCING HEIRARCHY (AS IT APPLIES TO POSTPRODUCTION:

Executive Producer: The ultimate boss, whose word can only challenged by the network. The EP oversees the entire machine and every aspect of the process.

Co-Executive Producer: A step below EP, the Co-EP generally shares many of the EP's responsibilities and authority but still serves at the pleasure of his or her direct superior.

Supervising Producer: An authority in the process, the Supervising Producer often oversees the day-to-day progress of the editorial team, while the EP and Co-EP may only step in for the most crucial creative decisions.

Senior Producer (or **Senior Story Producer**): This is often the most seasoned or experienced story producer on the team. He or she may help the Supervising Producer manage the bigger picture or may simply perform the same tasks as every other story producer but enjoy a slightly better title and perhaps a better salary.

Story Producer: This is the producer who most directly works with the editor on a day-to-day basis. Story producers are less in charge of the whole, but they're more responsible for whatever smaller parts their editors work on. Their responsibilities include building stringouts, helping with footage and interview searches, and noting an editor's work as it evolves.

Associate Producer: The AP is often a recently promoted production assistant. They are at the bottom of the story-producing ladder and are generally assigned the less glamorous tasks. Their responsibilities include: less crucial and more time-consuming footage searches, transcribing and formatting voice-over and interview pickup scripts, organizing and distributing field notes, etc. They are rarely involved in giving notes and are generally absent from screenings, unless they are there to simply learn and observe.

4. LEARN YOUR BOSS'S PET PEEVES

I know I've touched upon this already, but it's such a crucial part of your professional survival that it warrants elaboration.

First and foremost in building any edit is making a great scene. Tell the strongest story with the strongest structure in the strongest way possible. And I've spent more than half this book guiding you through how to do just that. But a close second to *making a great scene* is making a scene that appeals to the specific and subjective tastes of one very important person—YOUR BOSS.

Every executive producer has his or her "THING." There's always something, or maybe a few somethings, that might seem insignificant to you BUT for this individual are absolute deal breakers. It might be that your EP hates jazzy music cues or B-ROLL with lip flap (viewing a clip's image without audio, so that we see onscreen characters speak without hearing what they're saying). Perhaps there is a particular camera move that just irks him no end. Maybe he just hates dissolves. These can seem like small and inconsequential touches, but trust me, they are ANYTHING BUT inconsequential if they bother your boss! So learn all your boss's bugaboos. Heed them in each and every cut you deliver. It is amazing how dramatically this can affect an executive producer's opinion of an editor. I've had strong cuts trashed and weaker ones applauded, all due to how well I listened to and compensated for my boss's hang-ups

To quickly ferret out these hang-ups, seek the advice of editors who have been on the show longer than you or story producers who have already sat through the show's preliminary screenings. They probably know the boss's quirks and predilections. If you can't get this all-important info from the editors or the story producers, then listen very, very carefully as you get the EP's notes in your own screenings. Pay special attention to things that come up again and again. If an EP harps on the same seemingly inconsequential issue over and over, then you know that that's his thing!

The more thoroughly you attend to your EP's tastes, the more confidence your boss will have in you and your talents. He will think to himself, "This editor is great. He never has lip flap in his B-ROLL. He's a real pro!" This little trick has not only preserved my job time and again but has also led to many more jobs down the line.

5. DON'T ARGUE

Making television is a collaborative process. It takes many minds and many talents to construct a living, breathing piece of entertainment, especially one that is clear, concise, and broadcast worthy. But as important as it is to contribute throughout the process, it is equally important to always remember your place within it.

There are all sorts of EP's out there. Some are very confident, some less so. Some are more bullheaded and ego-driven. Others are more respectful and modest. Some executive producers will go out of their way to ask your opinion, and some will discourage it. But no matter what type of boss you have, and how much freedom you and your opinions are allowed, one thing is almost always true: *There is a time when enough is enough.* There is a point at which suggestion and debate teeter dangerously at the precipice of becoming a counterproductive argument. THIS would be the time to shut up, listen, and do what you're told.

You are an *employee.* You have been hired to help the EP do what HE wants, first and foremost. If you feel one way about some aspect of a cut, express that position, and if your boss clearly disagrees—shut up and do it his way. There will be many changes to your work along the way. Some changes you may strongly disagree with. Get used to it. You are only going to keep working if the people who pay you like working with you. This means that they feel you have a good attitude, can listen to and clearly interpret THEIR notes, and will deliver the show THEY want THEIR way.

I know this sounds a bit harsh, but believe me, it doesn't mean you aren't playing a huge creative role. At every step of the editorial process you are making key creative decisions. You are still authoring much of the finished product. But at the same time, you must always, always, always remember YOUR PLACE and be ready to defer to and accommodate those above you.

6. MANAGE YOUR TIME

"Good is great. Done is better!"

Jackson Anderer, Editor,
Extreme Makeover: Home Edition and *Celebrity Apprentice*

I have spent most of this book extolling the importance of taking the time to do your job right. When discussing music I stressed listening through as many cues as necessary to find the perfect match. When I discussed *Frankenbiting* I described how crucial it was to make each and every audio edit seamless and invisible to the ear. It is always important to do the very best job you can and to turn out the smoothest and strongest cuts possible. BUT you do not want to take TOO LONG to do it. Quality control is important. But time management is VITAL.

The last thing you want to be is the SLOW editor. You've probably heard the old saying *"Last hired, first fired."* In reality TV post a more apt adage might be *"Slowest on the show is the first editor to go!"*

You must always strike a balance between time and quality. You must know your project's deadline from the start and then set personal incremental deadlines for your work's progress. How much time do I have to look for this music cue? How much time can I spend looking for this interview bite? How long can I work at smoothing this cheat? Keep an eye on the clock, and let it help you make the hard choices about when to finesse and when to move on.

On a first rough cut, most producers don't fixate on the little stuff. They don't notice the imperfect cuts or the slightly bumpy audio edits. When they watch a cut for the first time they are looking to see if the story is clear. Is all the best stuff in there? Is everything moving at the right pace? For a first pass, you must nail CONTENT, CLARITY, PACING, and, most importantly, STORY. You will have time to polish your scene later. Sometimes, especially in a first cut, good enough really IS good enough.

Take Note: The Anxious Producer

There is an exception to what I just wrote above. Sometimes, when starting a new gig, you will be faced with a producer who is too high-strung to simply let you do your thing. Some producers NEED to know you're "good" before they can relax, breathe, and treat you like a normal human being. If you get a sense that this might be the case with the producer you are working for, then applying some early polish to your scene becomes more of a priority. A pretty good sign of an overly anxious or nervous producer is one who starts asking to see even the beginnings of your work much earlier than is reasonable. This sort of person might pop into your bay and say, *"Hey, show me something good."* Or he or she might ask one too many times, *"When can I see something?"* or *"How's it going? Do you want to show me anything?"* What does all this mean? It means that your job is not yet entirely secure. So what do you do? How do you ease a producer's jittery nerves while still managing your deadlines?

My approach is this:

Let's imagine I've been assigned a five-minute scene to edit, and it's become clear that I am working with a nervous producer who needs to be convinced of my skills. I will often spend more than enough time polishing and perfecting just *the first minute or so* of the scene. I will sacrifice the time I should be spending on other aspects of the cut and go overboard to make just this first bit as strong as possible.

Then, while we're still in the early stages of the edit process, I'll show this with the caveat, "I'm still in the midst, but here's what I have so far." Doing this can serve two ends. First, it can alleviate your producer's anxiety and win his or her trust. Second, it may actually buy you MORE time! As soon as your producer knows you have talent, he or she is going to want to give you the time you need to get your cut right. So, if you need a little extra time to perfect your cut, the producer who trusts you and believes that you're making something great will give it to you. After all, a strong first cut only makes the producer look good to his or her boss.

So, if you discover you are working with a Panicky Peter or a Second Guessing Sallie, polish just the first bit, calm their nerves, and then get back to time management as usual.

7. Branch Out

For better or worse, the job of a reality TV editor is a freelance one. A show usually lasts only a few months. And then you're on to your next one. You are essentially a professional nomad. For this reason, once you've established yourself as an editor on your first show at your first production company, once you've landed a real actual credit or two, it is then time to leave the nest. It's time to start spreading your wings, building your identity, and establishing your network. In short, it's time to BRANCH OUT. (NOTE: Another important reason to leave the nest is that the company that promoted you from an AE will often want to think of you as an AE. This is simply human nature. The only way to erase this stigma is to branch out by building your credits. Then, if you ever do return to the company where you worked as AE, you can do so on your own terms as a proven industry commodity.)

Okay, wonderful, but how exactly DO you branch out? Well, a good place to start is by looking within. The great thing about working in a freelance world is that you're not alone. All of your fellow reality TV editors are in the same position, and so are most reality TV producers. This is why your *networking* and *relationship building* don't stop when you become an editor. Instead, these activities need to increase tenfold. Bond with your coworkers, commiserate with and support them. Each and every job you land is a new opportunity to expand your network and your reputation.

Your future as an editor is absolutely 100 percent about WHO YOU KNOW. I can count on one hand how many times I've actually gone in for an interview or had my résumé references checked. Almost all of my jobs have come from direct referrals—from the recommendations of editors and producers whom I have worked with in the past. And, often, that recommendation is all that's been required to book my next gig.

On the Job:

You are nearing the end of your current job. Knowing that you need to book your next gig, you send out a mass email announcing your availability. One of the recipients is Jack, a producer you worked with last summer. Jack is currently working on *Hell's Kitchen*, and as luck would have it, one of *Kitchen*'s editors just quit. In order to stay on schedule, the show's executive producer gathers his trusted producers together and asks if anyone knows a good editor to step in. Jack raises his hand, mentions your name, and BINGO. The next thing you know you are getting a call from the series' post supervisor to discuss your rate and start date.

There is nothing stronger in this business than a *personal vouch*. Someone that the EP trusts vouches for you and says you're a rock star. That is the magic key to unlocking the door to almost every reality TV editing job.

Building new relationships and *keeping in touch* with colleagues you've worked with in the past is at the heart of maintaining a long and healthy editing career. I will sometimes organize gatherings of colleagues at my home or treat a group of them to dinner. I send holiday cards, birthday notes, and baby gifts to my business associates and friends, and I attend every function I am ever invited to. Facebook is great for this: It makes it easy to keep track of and check in on many former coworkers. LinkedIn can also be helpful in this way.

I would be nowhere without the many great friends I have made throughout my career, people who have had my back and pushed my name to the top of the hiring list. But remember, this is not a one-way street. You must always be ready to return the favor. We are, after all, a community. I have gotten many of my colleagues jobs, and will continue to do so whenever possible.

Quick Tip: Arrive Casually Late

When I'm invited to a large gathering like a party or BBQ, I often will arrive an hour after the invitation states, or even later. I hate being the first or second one at a party. All eyes are suddenly on me. I become a symbol for the success or failure of the entire event. I become the recipient of any and all stresses and insecurities the host might be feeling. How am I doing? Am I having fun? Do I want anything? I end up having to overcompensate and overperform just to keep the host's anxiety in check. At a party I like to slip through the crowd moving from conversation to conversation. I like to *work the room*, and not have the entire place watching and assessing my every move.

Just as arriving fashionably late for a simple social get-together can put you at ease, so can hiring on to a gig "fashionably late" (i.e., once it's already up and running with a good sense of itself) put you at ease in the workplace. As I've said before, the start of a new series is often a hotbed of second-guessing and finger pointing. Nobody knows what's what, and everyone is looking for someone else to blame. All too often an unsuspecting editor will find himself or herself the unwitting scapegoat and undeserving casualty of such disorder or confusion.

I look for jobs on shows that are well into their run, perhaps starting their second or third seasons, or which are at least past the early stressful freak-out stage. Firings are stressful for everyone. Even if you don't get fired, the simple psychological effects of seeing those around you getting axed raises your stress level way beyond where it should ever be. Also, by arriving in the wake of or well after a show's initial upheaval, your job can actually be more secure. Once a show goes through its growing-pains firings, such dismissals are not likely to happen again soon. The powers that be have gotten the whole firing and blame-shifting thing out of their system, and everybody is ready to just get to work and get the show done.

8. ROLL WITH THE PUNCHES

I have been lucky thus far: I have never been fired. But I know many great editors who have. And, more often than not, it had absolutely NOTHING to do with them or their work.

This is a freelance business, and being an independent contractor enables an employer to clip you on a whim, for no reason at all. This is simply something that you are going to need to reconcile with and prepare for. Understand that it is just part of the game. And, no, it doesn't mean the end of your career. It's nothing personal. Many have endured it and will continue to endure it. There is no perfect way to ALWAYS keep your job and to never get fired. Editors get fired. It happens.

If it does happen, if you are the unwitting victim of a superior's stresses, take a deep breath, relax, and remember that reality TV is an editor's market. There are a ton of jobs out there, and they are multiplying daily. I've actually seen editors get fired by an EP and hired within a week by another EP on another show at the same production company! That's how in-demand we are!

So if you get clipped, remember to *roll with the punches*. In some ways it's kind of a rite of passage. And once you've gone through it, you'll see that it's just another part of the game—nothing more.

• • •

So there are my pearls. This is what I know about getting the gig and keeping it. This is the knowledge that I've gleaned from being in the trenches, and it has served me well. It has helped me build a successful career that has continued to grow. I know it can do the same for you. So heed my advice, work hard, stay positive, and, most importantly, get ready to have a LOT of fun and make a LOT of money doing it!

CHAPTER 17 REVIEW

Choose the correct answers from the lettered list.

1. Once you've established yourself as an editor on your first show at your first production company, once you've landed a real actual credit or two, it is then time to what?

2. It is crucial to learn your bosses' ___ _____. Heed them in each and every cut you deliver. It is amazing how dramatically this can affect an executive producer's opinion of an editor.

3. When you step into a new job, there is one golden rule to remember: Never be afraid to ___ _____.

4. Quality control is important. But ____ _____ is VITAL.

5. If you are lucky enough to come onto a show midstream, the very first things you want to do are study and mimic the ____ _____.

6. If you feel one way about some aspect of a cut, express that position, and if your boss clearly disagrees ____ __ ___ __ __ ___ ___.

7. Building relationships and _____ __ _____ is at the heart of maintaining a long and healthy editing career.

   a. Shut up and do it his way
   b. Keeping in touch
   c. Branch out
   d. Earlier episodes
   e. Pet peeves
   f. Ask questions
   g. Time management

Answers: 1-c, 2-e, 3-f, 4-g, 5-d, 6-a, 7-b

FINAL WORD

Reality TV exploded into the American mainstream at the beginning of the 21st century. Almost overnight an industry was born, and with it came brand-new opportunities for wealth and success. Those opportunities continue to grow at an astounding rate and have remained unaffected by the economic struggles of our country and the world.

I feel very lucky to have stumbled into the job I have. I am a creative storyteller helping to define a new medium. My job is fun and challenging, and it pays HANDSOMELY! I want to share that opportunity with others. I cannot believe how untapped and undiscovered this vocation really is. The need for strong reality TV editors is great, and growing every day. I am constantly getting calls, and not only do I have to turn the jobs down, I can't even find someone to recommend. EVERYONE is working!!!

Reality TV editing is truly *the best-kept job secret in Hollywood*. And the dirtiest secret of all is that it's not really that hard to do. I mean, it's not easy, but it's not brain surgery either. It takes practice and time and focus, but you can get it down. You can learn the language. The rest is gravy.

Read this book. Read it again. Absorb the lessons. They are based on years of hands-on experience and success. I lived it so that you can have a head start on the competition. Get moving. Find that internship. Start climbing that ladder. I look forward to seeing you in the bays. Let's start making television together. I mean, to be perfectly honest, I need someone to start recommending for all those jobs out there. Let's make it you.

Acknowledgments

Special thanks to Carol Saunders, Brent Kinetz, Sax Eno, Joe Talbot Hall, Bill Marin, Bevin McNamara, Jesse Willenbring, The Sunset People, Jim Fox, Gwen Feldman, Sabrina Mar, Jackson Anderer, Tim Roche, Aaron Simard, Anthony Rivard, Juan Pablo Prieto, Autumn Doerr, George Dybas, Cindy Scott, Jeff Seidman, Pavel Dyban, Vincent Ueber, Alex Robinson, Scott Bagley, Rachel Katz, Andrew Bernstein, Peter Beren, Heather Dawson, Alice Alexander, Jasper Alexander, Darren Bader, Peter Delman, Al Romano, Jayson Haedrich, Al Goldyne, Tamara Badgely-Horowitz, Richard Horowitz, John Babinec, Steve Sharlet, Paul Heiman, Brian Zagorsky, Rusty Austin, Paul Buccieri, Hans Schiff, Tim Puntillo, and AVID technology.